# Nine Deadly Venoms

## ...staying alive in the 21st Century

*"Driven by some primitive and passionate energy, she
revealed the nine deadly venoms. 'Conquer them and you
live forever, but beware!' she said with a wicked leer.
'Each one is indeed a venom, the worst kind of poison,
and is very, very deadly."*

**ALEX GORDON**

# Nine Deadly Venoms

## ...staying alive in the 21st Century

Author: Alex Gordon

Ebuilders Ltd
5 & 6 The Azure Suites,
Churchill Court,
112 The Street,
Rustington,
W Sussex BN16 3DA
UK

www.ninedeadlyvenoms.com

Nine Deadly Venoms

...staying alive in the 21st Century

Author: Alex Gordon

Original Subtitle: The autobiography of an urban shaman

Copyright © Alex Gordon

\* \* \*

Special Note: Within the book you will find quotations by various individuals. Just because we have included the quotation here does not mean that the author endorses everything that these individuals may have said or done.

Published by Ebuilders Ltd

ISBN – 0-9546496-0-5

First Edition

# Contents

# Nine Deadly Venoms
# – A Book Of Discovery

Nine Deadly Venoms has a powerful and compelling message about the considerable hurdles that we all must overcome if we are to move to a better level of existence. As a 'self help' book, it will inspire and enlighten. Light bulbs will flick on in your head as you realise why things have been the way they are and why you have experienced the life you have.

Whilst written in an autobiographical manner, Nine Deadly Venoms is not your usual autobiography. The autobiographical nature of the writing is just a "tool" to explain the Nine Deadly Venoms – the Nine Deadly Venoms that human kind must overcome.

Nine Deadly Venoms is about evolving. It is about facing our fears and overcoming them. The author explains and guides but can offer no shortcuts, for it is only by making the journey ourselves that we will find the answers.

Nine Deadly Venoms is also about the return of the Matriarchal Age and, in particular, the return of Lilith. It is Lilith who explains the Nine Deadly Venoms to Alex Gordon. It is through knowledge of the Nine Deadly Venoms and avoiding them that we can quite literally live the life of our dreams.

This book signposts the changing of the ages.

Very importantly for the male sex, it should be noted that the Matriarchal Age is not about feminism. It is about doing things in the right order, the natural way. Matriarchal Man is far stronger than Patriarchal Man!

It would not be appropriate at this time to suggest that knowledge of the Nine Deadly Venoms is comparable to say the knowledge of the Ten Commandments but there cannot be much doubt that the "lessons for life" revealed are invaluable and impacting for a great many people. Our wish is that you are one of them. Ultimately the journey is yours. This book is just a signpost. Times are changing and the days of the negative, evil people are numbered.

Ebuilders Ltd – Publishers

"And there appeared a great wonder in heaven, a woman clothed with the sun, and the moon under her feet, and upon her head a crown of twelve stars."

Revelation 12:1

# THE CHILDHOOD SHOWS
# THE MAN

# AS MORNING SHOWS THE DAY

John Milton

# Chapter One

## *That thing in the cellar is not my Mother!*

I was born on 6th June 1949 in Swindon, just after midnight. Spooky! Possible occult significance? There was no crossfire hurricane, but it was raining. I was the largest baby ever born in that maternity hospital and the nurses nicknamed me Bruce Woodcock (a heavyweight boxing champion of the time). I was a greedy baby and took all the calcium out of my mother so that all her teeth eventually fell out. I took all the water and vitamins and proteins, too. Yes, I got my share, all right, but needless to say my mother never had any more children. Then I went to sleep for four years.

When I was four years old, I remember playing with a tin-plate paddle steamer in the bath. I don't remember anything else until I was six, so I must have fallen asleep again. I still love beds and sleep and the night and dreams. Getting into bed is like being wrapped up in a warm purple blanket by some all-knowing night nurse who strokes your forehead and whispers soft compliments and sweet nothings until sleep comes – and dreams are such fun! You can drive whatever car you like, be the fastest gunfighter in the west (like Robert Vaughn in The Magnificent Seven), make love to anyone you like, eat what you like, be Robin Hood or King

Arthur. Yes, dreams are great fun, and before you go all stiff on me, don't tell me you've never had a fantasy!

When I was six I decided to do something with my life. I wanted to be proactive and upwardly mobile. My father worked on the railways; everyone in Swindon worked on the railways. He worked long hours for very little money and was a big, strong man who was as gentle as a lamb, even though he could bang nails in with his fist if he happened to drop his hammer.

My mother was from Yorkshire and she cleaned and cooked and scrubbed and polished everything, and still had to pander to my needs. Bless her. Who'd be a mother? Not me, that's why I chose to be born a boy, and a spoilt one at that; no sharing for me. I didn't just shove my siblings out of the nest, I made sure they never got into the nest in the first place. Then we moved house.

We moved into an aluminium bungalow, one of those homes fit for heroes that the government threw up just after the war so that everyone could be happy again. It was boiling hot in summer and freezing cold in winter. It had a large garden in which my father grew all his own vegetables, a big living room where we had coal fires and watched early black-and-white television, a large kitchen with a big table on which my mother punched and slapped pastry around, a cold bathroom, windows that misted up ... and a concentration of negative energy as black as the pit.

This 'thing' moved around. Up and down the wide, gloomy hall between the living room and the kitchen, into the bathroom and bedrooms. I could see it, like the smoke of a burning tyre, about the size of a dustbin lid. I could smell it, a psychic smell, worse than anything you can imagine. I could sense it, as a destroyer captain senses a submarine; and it was a nasty piece of work, a malignant force.

No-one else could see it or smell it or sense it except me – but they could sure as hell feel it. My mother used to wake up in the small hours screaming and crying that someone was trying to suffocate her. My father would venture into the bathroom in the middle of the night and run out again, his face white. They never spoke about it, but they felt it.

Sometimes it would venture into my bedroom. I could sense it moving around the bed – waiting, watching and playing a game. Pets sickened and died, my father had two serious operations, everything went wrong. One night my grandmother came down from Yorkshire and I stayed up to see her; it was the night Buddy Holly and the Big Bopper were killed in a plane crash. She brought me an old wind-up gramophone and it was nice to see her. As she chatted with my parents in the living room, 'it' was in the hall. I could sense it on my radar, the radar in my head that I was born with, part of standard issue equipment for high spirits such as myself. It was waiting and wondering, 'Is this a new victim?'.

I became too scared to go to sleep. I had ten cuddly toys in the bed with me, and I used to make a tent in the bed using my mother's copper stick as a tent-pole. There all eleven of us would sit with three torches, waiting, waiting for the temperature to drop, waiting for the goose-bumps to come on my skin. I waited, the teddy bears waited, the panda waited – we all waited, each as dumb as the other. Sometimes far away I could hear my parents talking in the living room, but the hall seemed as wide as the Grand Canyon and as dark as a coalmine and the light switch was at the far end near the front door. My father had started to work nights by then. I would hear him say goodbye to my mother and cycle off to make the big steam engines in the factory – the factory full of fires, molten metal fires –then he would be gone. My mother would go to bed, and 'it' would start to move around, examining things, stroking things, like some sick octopus. When I was eight, my father became ill again. He had a perforated eardrum that bled and drove him mad with pain and he had to go into hospital where the doctors were going to try and graft a piece of flesh from his thigh over the perforation. He was terrified, standing with his suitcase in Reception at the hospital, a grim, dark building full of cream tiles and painted pipes. I wanted him to come home there and then, but he couldn't; he had to go through with it. The next time I visited him he was unconscious and with enough bandages around his head to wrap an Egyptian mummy. I took him some grapes, which he couldn't eat, of course, and some Lucozade, which he couldn't drink, and a sexy book, which he couldn't read.

We came home. I went to bed with my ten stuffed brothers-in-arms. I thought of my father lying there and of my Blue Persian cat that was sick and dying in a box in the living room. I thought of my mother trying to sleep with the light on and half a ton of lucky charms around the bed. I thought of all the things that had gone wrong in that house. Then, at just gone midnight, 'it' decided to prowl the house again. I felt it moving past the bedroom door, mocking, laughing, feeding off all the fear, and for the first time in my life I felt anger. I got mad. I realised that I could either just 'take it' or fight and I decided to fight. An eight-year-old boy versus ... what? Damned if I knew. I held my first conference of war with my ten senior officers; I'd woken up now. No more sleeping my life away. It was time for fighting.

The next morning I went into town and bought a toy double-barrelled flintlock pistol, a toy pirate pistol and some caps. I inserted two caps, one for each barrel, and took it into the nearest church, placed it on the altar when no-one was looking, then I sat down on a cold, hard, polished pew and prayed. I didn't know what I was praying to – God, Great Spirit, the Universe, Allah, whoever was up there, whoever was more powerful than me, which seemed to be everything and everybody. The forlorn figure of Christ gazed down at me from the cross and an old lady shuffled into the church and started arranging flowers. I waited for a sign, a signal, but none came. My bottom was sore and I was cold. I picked up the gun and left.

I realised that the 'thing' in the house was composed of energy. The only way I could hope to destroy it was by being more powerful, being able to generate more energy. No god was going to do it for me. There was a notice outside the church showing the times when God was in and when, presumably, he was resting. I figured even God had to rest; it had to be hard work creating worlds and star systems. I remember my young Sunday school teacher, who seemed very sweet and innocent even to me, as a child. She gave me little perfumed pictures of Jesus doing this and that and told me that if I was good, God would look after me. She always seemed so vulnerable and I always prayed that her dreams would come true. Even though I didn't believe in praying, she did, so I guessed it might work for her.

I tried to tell her about the thing in the house, hoping for the support of her prayers, but she didn't believe me. She thought I was cute but that I was imagining things, but even then I knew that my spirit was bigger than hers, and stronger. I might have had the little body of a boy, but inside I was a warlord and even then I knew that I was destined to do battle with what I came to call 'shadow' energies.

In the tent that was my bed, every night I held my little gun between my hands and tried to empower the tiny amount of explosives in the caps. I imagined white light blazing from my hands and concentrated my eyes on to the caps, attempting to laser them and fill them with power, and, little by little, I could feel it starting to work. The gun resided under my pillow, safe and warm and dry, awaiting the night of the final conflict.

Days came and went, shifting between the 'real world' of school, behaving myself, washing behind my ears, eating meals, homework, and my personal psychic world. One thing I learnt here is that the psychic world dictates the so-called 'real world'. If you get it wrong inside your head it will all be wrong outside your head. The second thing I learnt was that if you want to survive, to be happy, peaceful and free, to have those things that everyone yearns for, then you have to fight. You have to fight yourself, fight your own fear. There are no excuses. Excuses are a way of avoiding fighting. If you don't fight, then something or someone will make you run away from life and you'll never get the peace, the happiness or the freedom. You'll live on the run. It is OK to be scared. Everyone gets scared. Even Jesus got scared, but you have to fight. Fight your own fear.

I swear that the 'thing' in the house knew what I was doing. The atmosphere became even more heavy and oppressive. My father came home from hospital, his head still swathed in bandages; he was confined to bed and he was always in pain. The house seemed to grow colder. The Persian cat was still alive but having to be fed on warm milk. My mother looked thin and pale and I was tired. I knew time was running out and I had to make a move. I decided to wait till the next full moon to make that move.

It was 22nd April, a few minutes after midnight. The moon illuminated my bedroom curtains. My stomach ached and I felt cold and panicky as I sat in my tent-bed

trying to build up my courage and put one last ounce of
energy into the pistol. This was The Night of the Hunter
(Robert Mitchum, black-and-white film, 1949, brilliant
film – child versus man – but this was different ... child
versus what?)

It was the strangeness of the enemy that turned my
stomach. It was the psychic smell, which I still smell
sometimes and which causes me to sit bolt upright in
bed, sweating and reaching for my cigarettes. It was so
different, you see. Even an alien fictional image is the
product of someone's imagination, but this was light-
years away from my mind, my consciousness and my
perceptions. I thought I was the hunter, but was I? Was I
really the prey? All of a sudden I felt like a stupid kid
with a toy pistol playing with fire and I was scared.

My ten silent comrades thought I could do it. Ratty did
it when he marched into the Wild Wood in The Wind in
the Willows to confront the stoats and the weasels as he
searched for his friend Mole, and I had to do it. There was
no-one else. Beyond the tent-bed there was the black
void, which wove itself into the black void of fear in my
mind. The void of unknown things.

It was a point of testing in my life. I could have just
continued to stay there scared night after night, hoping
that we might move, or I could have just watched sadly
as things got worse. I could have suffered, given in and
surrendered.

But I knew two things. First, I knew that it was
important to recognise these times as moments when the
Universe watches closely to see what you will do.
Second, it was important not to let yourself down in the
eyes of your ancestors, both genetic and spiritual, for the
point of conflict has been placed before you, so YOU can
make a difference. The Universe employs you and you
are the officer on the scene of the crime and this is why

no archangel appeared before me when I sat in the church. I was the instrument of change!

I jumped out of my bed into the dark and the cold. The chilly air wrapped itself around me instantly and the darkness filled me with imaginary monsters drawn from old films and books, each embellished by my own fears. I took a deep breath, held the little gun before me and slowly pulled back both hammers. I swear I could see a faint blue light around it; maybe that was wishful thinking, but I've read that elfin weapons glow green or blue in the presence of negativity.

As my eyes adjusted to the gloom, I began to make out the shapes of doors and windows. I could not switch on a light. This was a battle with the darkness in the darkness. I would fight the battle on my enemy's territory. I opened my bedroom door and moved out into the dark hallway. There was a faint glow of light to my right as the moon shone through a small pane of glass in the front door and that was all.

The hallway seemed vast and high as a cathedral. My radar was on full red alert but I could not detect anything unusual. I moved across the hall, opened the door to the living room and crossed over into the kitchen and back again into the hall. 'It' must be hiding, I thought. It must have made itself small, very small. My skin developed goose-bumps through my own imaginings. My feet felt frozen as I moved down the hall towards my parents' bedroom door, reached out for the round brass handle and then – all hell broke loose.

My radar screamed like a destroyer whooping its attack signal. Cold shivers shot up and down my spine and for a split second I was frozen in space and time, for 'it' was coming in on me from 'behind', from the front door. It had been secreting itself outside the house. In an instant, I realised my error of logic; the thing lived in the land around the house rather than in the house itself. I spun around and something or someone seemed to say, 'Don't pull the trigger, wait! It wants you to waste energy.' Then a black ball of energy shot past my right side, angry, merciless, cruel, leaving a nauseating psychic smell behind it as it disappeared into the bathroom. There it waited as if saying, 'Come and get me if you can, let's finish it.'

My radar screamed its warning. A blue light glowed from the little gun as I pushed open the bathroom door – and there it was, clear and visible for the first time. An ever-changing shape of blackness, so black, it was like a hole in the air, with a deep red heart pulsating at its centre, and it had become big, almost as big as the room. It hit me with a wave of nausea that made me screw up my eyes and feel sick. I sensed it was enjoying the confrontation, feeding off my fear, growing bigger and more powerful by the minute. I knew I should have laughed, as that would have killed the power source, but I was fighting an overwhelming urge to run. Just run away and keep running; my face was too frozen with fear to laugh and a thousand thoughts were flooding in on me. I was alone, in the dark, with some unspeakable thing and here I would die, or worse.

I raised the gun and, holding it with both hands, I aimed at the dark red heart of the thing and fired. At the same moment, it darted to my right, there was a red flash from the gun and a projectile of blue light hit the energy from just left of centre. It recoiled and turned in upon itself, as if experiencing a living organism's pain. Although this shot had succeeded in blowing away at least one third of its form, it was still able to move straight towards me for one last attack, one last attempt to overpower me with its foul energy.

19

I fired again and, this time, the beam of light caught it dead centre and it vanished into thin air. All was still, I could breathe easily again; the bathroom became brighter and the moonlight from the pane of glass in the front door began to illuminate the whole hallway and the air began to smell sweet. All the noise had awakened my parents, so I hurried back to bed and remained motionless until all was quiet again. Shortly after, I slipped outside and was violently sick in the garden.

It wasn't long after this event that we moved house. My father's luck had changed for the better. Not only did the local council offer us a house, but his operation, although not successful, healed well and the Blue Persian cat recovered. I could sit at the top of stairs in the middle of the night without the slightest twinge of fear or anxiety. The new house was peaceful and psychically clean.

Years later my father told us that we had only been allocated the 'dreaded bungalow' because no-one else could stay there for more than a few weeks. He was warned about its melancholy character but our need for a place to live had outweighed his reservations. Later I discovered that a gypsy had cursed the whole area. Why, I don't know, but I had learnt my first important shamanic lesson and that was that 'There is no evil outside of human intention'.

Never underestimate human intention!

AND WE ARE HERE AS ON

A DARKLING PLAIN

SWEPT WITH CONFUSED

ALARMS OF STRUGGLE

AND FLIGHT

WHERE IGNORANT ARMIES

CLASH BY NIGHT

Matthew Arnold

# Chapter Two

## *Red Alligators rule, OK?*

Whenever my mother suffered a migraine headache she would take my hand and place it on her forehead, and her pain would go away. I thought this was awfully clever of me and that everyone could do it. It was quite a shock when I realised that not everyone could.

I was at senior school now. Image was everything – street cred vital. I was not especially physical, being rather tall and thin, so I learnt to make up for my lack of power with brains, skill and cunning. I was also terrified of being trapped in a working-class lifestyle and had great dreams of rescuing my parents from their situation. Education became my goal and I plunged myself into learning with an absolutely insatiable appetite for knowledge. It wasn't always easy and I had to avoid all the usual school petty politics. Avoid being beaten up by the resident junior thugs, be the perfect diplomat, plus avoid getting my clothes, schoolwork, briefcase and looks ruined. But this, too, was a good learning process in its own right.

I still had recurrent nightmares from the experiences of earlier years, but the school was big and airy with huge windows that let in lots of light. The facilities were excellent and it was like my second home. Most of all, the teachers were the best group of people ever gathered together in one place. I adored and respected them all.

They became my role models and have remained so until this day, although I have now added Arnold Schwarzenegger, Robert Mitchum and Alan Rickman to the list.

Each one taught an academic subject but, more than that, they taught us lessons about life for anyone with eyes to see and ears to hear. I was sad that other children didn't seem to appreciate them as much as I did. 'Other children' could be divided into two groups: those who wanted to learn and progress and those who wanted to mess around and be a nuisance to everyone else. To protect myself from the latter, I formed a gang called the 'Red Alligators', 'red' because that is the colour of passion and anger.

This gang was formed from boys like myself who wanted to get on with life and learn as much as possible while being protected against the school goblins. It is very easy to underestimate goblins. When one is a child, the goblins have big thick skulls and great big fists. They're not usually very bright, but they move fast and can inflict enormous damage in a very short time.

Sometimes I wonder if parents fully realise just how terrifying these goblins can be to a child. To begin with, they should try getting down on their knees to view the world from a child's perspective. That way they might begin to understand how awesome the bullies can be. Also, goblins are pack creatures; they chase their prey in a fixed hunting pattern, surround it, hit and kick at it, until it can no longer run, and the black eyes, cut lips and smashed teeth are stark evidence, for weeks on end, that the victim couldn't run fast enough. Other children tend to laugh at the plight of the victims as a form of sympathetic magic which might ward off the same fate. Also, such grudging support creates some pride in their negative achievement in the tiny minds of the bullies and makes them less likely to turn on their supporters. A bullied child is a very lonely child. Teachers cannot really help and nor can parents, simply because they can't be there all the time.

The bullies will get you in the end, but pack creatures are very wary of other packs; they tend to seek out weak, solitary, defenceless prey and the Red Alligators became a very mean pack! 'Yea, though we walk through the valley of the shadow of death, we will fear no evil, because we're the meanest sons of bitches in the whole damned valley' was our motto. We tried once to translate it into Latin, but none of us could, mainly because the school didn't teach Latin. This was definitely a working-class survival-of-the-fittest school!

I must just mention the lone bully, the bully who is so hard, so thick and so nasty that he doesn't need a pack. He hunts alone. He is usually seriously mentally disturbed and everyone steers well clear of him. He is the most dangerous creature in the school and has even been known to attack teachers. Don't even attempt to take him on unless there are at least ten of you. He grows up without any discipline until he changes from a nasty piece of work in a small body into an even nastier piece of work in a large body. Eventually he ends up in a prison or mental institution, but until some judge eventually sends him away for ever he can do an awful lot of damage. Remember – there is no evil outside of human intention.

The image of the Red Alligators was totally contrived; a simple mask behind which we could get on with learning. Also, we regularly helped out weaker boys, protected them and at times became almost chivalrous. If we were attacked, we would hit back, divide and conquer and then punish each captive. Sometimes they were buried up to their necks in the sandpit or frog-marched down a very steep, grassy bank on to the hard tarmac path or just slapped around a bit or fined.

The worst punishment was being sellotaped naked to the girls' netball cage ten minutes before a girls' sports period. We achieved a very good non-reoffending rate. Following the motto of the New York Police Department, 'To Protect and Serve', we started off protecting and serving ourselves; then, as our confidence grew, we extended this to protect and serve other children until eventually we attempted to protect and serve the whole school.

Most of the pack goblins took to beating themselves up. Good is constant, but evil is compulsive, it cannot stop. For example, using the analogy of wolves in a sheep-pen, the wolves will eat all the sheep and then eat each other until the last wolf will gnaw away at itself. This is the way of evil. The art of chivalry is to save as many sheep as possible. This is a gross slander on wolves, which are indeed very beautiful creatures, but I need the analogy, so I hope the wolves will forgive me.

If you are a parent and your child is bullied and it starts to make his or her life a misery, please ... take assertiveness lessons, learn Kung Fu, go into the school and raise hell! Stop the damage at source because bullying certainly wrecks lives. It is better to be frowned upon for being overly forceful than allow your child to spend his or her whole life in therapy. Don't complain to the teachers, discipline the bully and if the parents complain ... discipline them too!

On average people use about two per cent of their brains – the rest is fear. Not the intense phobic fear, but the subtle kinds. Fear of not fitting in, not being good enough, not being liked, fear of getting it wrong, fear of time, age, sickness and death – the list is endless, and fear is like a fog that clouds our seeing and wrecks our enjoyment of life. The more fear a person has, the tighter will be his or her comfort zone.

The lone bully, for example, will perceive a simple innocent 'hello' as a threat and react accordingly. Small wonder that such people become more and more isolated, but these people are in effect the dunces of the universe, using perhaps as little as 0.2 per cent of their brains. And before all you New-Agers out there start shouting, 'Judgmental git!', 'Fascist!', 'Everyone is part of the greater whole', 'Cast him out into the bog of the eternal stench', I'm sorry, but we are talking here of people who have had perhaps eighty to ninety lifetimes and have learnt absolutely nothing and who make higher beings weary and bore them to death.

How would you like to wait seven hundred years for someone to do an act of kindness for the first time and be disappointed over and over again? Angels, so called, do not have an easy time. Of course everyone is part of the greater whole, it's just that some people play a bigger part than others do. The potential is there for everyone but, without kind actions, potential is just an intellectual concept.

The Universe is a very hard creation to run and to organise and it would be nice if everyone played a part in helping it along.

Yes, we do have evil spirits and we have very lazy spirits – and they all inhabit human bodies. They live in houses, streets and in towns and cities all over the world. You might even know one or two! Again, there is no evil outside of human intention.

\* \* \*

Back to school. Having achieved a semblance of peace and order, I could now get on with the difficult job of learning. I was not especially bright, but I found I could make up for that lack with hard work. I think I drove the teachers mad asking them questions and making demands on their time, but they were very kind and never refused me.

There was Mr Powell, my long-suffering physics teacher who, presumably to avoid being bombarded by my questions, took me off in his old Austin A40 to spend a day in Harwell. It was there that I discovered the particle accelerator and the cyclotron, and the microcosm of atomic particles and nuclear physics opened up to me. It was light-years more fun than any theme park, to be able to see matter in motion, and the memory of seeing such mysteries is still vivid today.

More than teaching me physics, though, he taught me that it doesn't matter what sort of background you come from (he'd had a particularly bad one himself), you can still 'make it', still reach for the stars, still make of yourself whatever you wish or dream or want to be. He taught me that there was a big, beautiful universe out there and all one needs to enjoy it is the will to try and the innocence to dream bold dreams. He taught me to see beyond the mundane and to go beyond conditioning; to try that little bit harder to win the prize – which might be a glimpse of Sirius, the realisation of some profound truth or someone's grateful smile or kind look. Prizes come in many forms, as do angels.

Mr Packer was our English teacher, a big powerful man. No-one argued with him, unless he was either Bruce Lee or totally insane! A couple of boys did try, but I believe they're still in therapy.

Mr Packer had a heart as big as the sun and twice as warm. He taught me how to use words to create beauty and to convey beauty instead of just conveying needs and desires; how to paint word pictures, the meaning of words, what strange interesting things they actually are and how taken for granted they are. Words were his life. He could mix them up and create something beautiful in the same way someone can combine ingredients and make a beautiful cake.

He also taught me the down side, that words in the wrong mind, the ill-intentioned mind, or on the wicked tongue, could be a more deadly weapon than any bullet. He always urged you to think before speaking and to make the thinking as kind and as fair as possible without, of course, being weak.

Mr Packer was anything but weak. He had been a Spitfire pilot during the Second World War. Often after school had finished he would tell me enthralling stories of being hurled skywards and of being tossed around in the clouds behind a roaring Merlin engine; of streaking out of the clouds behind and above some lone German bomber, holding its fate for a second on the twitch of his thumb, then hearing the rattle of machine-gun fire; seeing the bomber lurch and smoke and dip like an injured whale and spiral down, ever down, then pulling his plane skywards again, towards the sun, like Icarus.

Again, he was careful to tell me the down-side, of one moment flying as if in heaven, watching the sun flashing on the cockpit, then suddenly being hit and spiralling out of control. Fire, panic, terror, incredible pain, in a world spinning over and over. Battling like a robot to free the cockpit cover, climbing out and trying to activate his parachute with burnt hands. Drifting to earth beneath a canopy of silk to land exhausted and terrified on England's green and pleasant land.

He urged me always to appreciate silence, stillness, peace, serenity and tranquillity, for in stillness, wisdom comes, answers come, inspiration comes, and if you can dare to dream of where the wisdom comes from, you are already halfway to seeing heaven on earth.

He urged me always to reach out to the greater universal mind; it is stronger, wiser and kinder than one's own. It will protect you and sustain you. It will bless your friends and confound your enemies and will love you as you've never been loved before. When I asked him what this force was called, he replied, 'It has many names – best call it the joy of being alive!'.

Mr Ricketts was our physical education teacher. He looked like a stand-in for a Greek god – tall, blond, muscular and confident. He once wrote 'pathetic' on my school report as a comment on my physical ability and I have to admit he was being generous rather than simply fair.

On our first encounter in his office, he smiled benignly and placed a cigarette paper on his desk.

'Right,' he said, 'now try to move that with your mind.' Like an idiot I did try, but of course it did not move. 'OK,' he said, his right cheek twitching with annoying glee, 'now try and move it with your feelings.'

I was getting mad now, so I just folded my arms and glared at him.

'Oh, don't quit yet.' he said. 'You are the school genius, after all. Try once more and, this time, try and move it with your spirit.'

'Stuff you,' I replied contemptuously.

'Tut tut and thrice tut,' he said (for he was also a comedian). 'Do I detect a weakness, a lack in your abilities?'

I stayed silent, not wishing to push my luck. He picked up the cigarette paper and rolled it into a tiny ball between his fingers and tossed it – ping – into the litter bin.

'You see,' he went on, 'the physical body is important, it can do many, many things that other aspects cannot do, and that is what you're going to learn from me and,' he added with a chilly tone, 'whether you like it or not, Einstein.'

From then on there were three periods of hell every week. I failed to reach the sandpit in the long jump, went under the bar in the high jump, dropped the shot on my foot, half-drowned in the swimming pool, suffered a panic attack halfway up the gymnasium wall bars, threw the ball away and adopted the foetal position in a game of rugby and was almost knocked unconscious by a cricket ball. I learnt to hate Mr Ricketts with the ferocity of a forest fire.

He would run along beside me as I puffed and panted around the running track, saying, 'Don't worry, Einstein, it's only your sub-atomic particles becoming energised.'

He would bounce medicine balls off my stomach until I was almost sick, saying, 'One day, some woman will thank me for this.' (I didn't understand what he meant at the time.) He would hold me under water to get me used to the idea of drowning.

I played football in four feet of snow, I fell exhausted on ten-mile cross-country runs. I was battered and bruised by soft balls, hard balls, round balls and oval balls. Laughed at, jeered at, insulted. Until one day, the light of understanding suddenly shone through my brain. I got mad! I got mad at the start of a fencing lesson for which I'd been picked out as the practice dummy. Yet as soon as I felt the sword in my hand, something told me I'd held one before. I'd found my element at last and a great excitement welled up inside me. It was as familiar to me as my forefinger. Nothing could stop me now! After a heated period of fierce exchanges, I chased Mr Ricketts out of the gymnasium and around the playing field, prodding him all the time in the backside with my sabre.

'Now you've got it,' he exclaimed, obviously delighted.

'Got what?' I asked, as I pondered on whether to run him through or not.

'Aggression,' he said. 'Power, determination, will or, as the Welsh would call it, hwyl – can't do anything without it.'

I went on to be a county record javelin thrower and a formidable miler. Mr Ricketts married a very attractive art teacher and I bought him a portable hi-fi system as a wedding present. Inside the accompanying card I wrote, 'With humble and grateful thanks for all your effort, time, patience, energy and wisdom'.

I was honoured to be taught by all my teachers, but Mr Finch-Crisp, the metalwork teacher, taught me the most profound lesson of all. I was hopeless at metalwork, but he didn't mind; he accepted that one could not be good at everything and he seemed to like me as a person and would spend many hours chatting to me over cups of tea after school hours.

Mr Finch-Crisp had hair as white as snow, even though he was only middle-aged. He had no fingernails and his bottom lip curved painfully over his chin, making speech very difficult for him. His face was lined and worn with pain and his spirit was very, very tired. He'd been a victim of a Japanese POW camp in the war and the brave and gallant knights of Bushido had slowly pulled out his fingernails and pushed red-hot needles through his lips and the shock and fear of it all had turned his hair white overnight.

Having barely survived the Japanese, he now had to suffer school bully-boys, the thugs who carried on where the knights of Bushido had left off and every day, unrelentingly, made his life hell.

They would smash into the metalwork workshop like deranged barbarians, mock him, deride him, imitate him, then take armfuls of tools and drop them into the blowtorch tray and burn off all the handles, always wrecking, destroying, hurting. They showed not a trace of compassion or remorse; it was all good fun to them and I learnt to hate them and to hate the Japanese and to plot revenge on them all, but his perceptions were well ahead of me.

One evening he said to me, 'If you hate, they have won – they have made you like themselves. They are young spirits, fearful of life and death. They do not understand what they do and if I can forgive them, then it is not for you to dishonour me by hating on my behalf; that is not friendship.

'If you would be my friend, a true friend, then listen to what I say and maybe you can carry forward the good things that I know. I have lived my destiny. I hope that my next life will be much easier. I am not a brave man, but I have won through. Now you must win through also and your best weapon is wisdom.'

I became very upset and said, 'Why does God, the Universe, whatever it may be, allow such cruelty?'

'It doesn't,' he answered with a smile. 'People have free will, and sometimes they make wrong choices. I was a victim of their wrong choices and, though this may be hard for you to understand, they gave me a great gift.' He leaned forward, fixed me with his clear, sparkling blue eyes, and whispered, 'Listen and learn. All life is sacred, all life is precious and all life is inter-linked. 'God' is not outside of you, it is within you and within all life itself.

'If you love, cherish and uplift any life form, you will enhance yourself – but if you hate, destroy or ridicule any life form, you will surely suffer the same fate yourself, because you are bound to them all by the strands of sacred energy. A leaf is as precious as you, so is an insect; animals are your teachers, the earth is a living being – hurt nothing, save and rescue and reach out to whatever you see in your life's path that is in trouble and you will be blessed.'

I thought deeply about what he had said over the next few weeks. I wrestled with my feelings. One moment my mind caught a glimpse of the peace that his philosophy contained and the next moment I was filled with thoughts of hate and revenge and retribution.

One evening, after class, he called me over to him and invited me to stay behind, which I was of course pleased to do. He made two mugs of tea with hands that trembled as they always did; he passed me my tea and sat down opposite me. 'Listen carefully,' he said and I did, for I had the greatest respect for him.

'Soon I will die,' he said in a calm, level voice, 'but do not be sad, it is time for me to go home. This body will return to dust and my spirit will move on fitter and wiser and stronger, ready for whatever the universe wishes me to do next. No-one ever dies, we are all immortal, we just don't realise it. It just means that you won't be able to touch me for a while but then, unless you can touch a person's spirit, the gesture is mostly meaningless.' He smiled and sipped his tea with difficulty.

'Now listen,' he said, 'listen and "inwardly digest", as they say. It is not time that makes people old, it is the negative energy with which people pollute one another. The negative energy of hate, resentment, need, guilt and fear is like radiation. When you are faced with it, it enters your body and slows down the reproductive cycle of your cells. All cells reproduce themselves, but if the energy frequency is slowed down some cells lie dormant; they do not reproduce and then we have lines on our faces and failing organs, which we then call "age".

'I suspect that one day you will find the secret of removing that energy and, if you ever do, you will be able to heal the sick and give people back their youth.

Our bodies do not wear out as everyone assumes. They are constantly reproducing themselves, but if they are polluted, the cells will reproduce the pollution also so nothing is gained. Learn how to get rid of the pollution – and that is why I've never cared that you can't make a garden fork or a coal shovel. That is not your purpose in this life!'

Two weeks later he died and I cried. I sat in the middle of the school field wishing to be alone. Fluffy clouds played across the blue sky, a cool breeze caressed my face, birds dipped and hovered as if playing with the wind, the sun burnt down wild and fierce and brave and seemed to encourage the luminous green grass to grow stronger. I knew he was out there somewhere and I knew he was happy. So although I was sad because I missed him, I knew I had to cherish his gifts and build on them, never forget them and one day, maybe, in my own small way, I would make him happier still.

THERE IS NO GOOD

IN ARGUING WITH THE
INEVITABLE.

THE ONLY ARGUMENT
AVAILABLE

WITH AN EAST WIND IS

TO PUT ON YOUR OVERCOAT

James Russel Lowell

# Chapter Three

## *Jane*

I was high on testosterone when I left school to take my place on the great stage of life. I had a brain the size of a planet and I had no fear. I was full of high ideals and virtues and I was going to carry the flag of goodness into the big wide world and change everything and everyone around to create Utopia. Little did I know that lurking beneath all my pomp and circumstance was a lot of shyness, zero sexual experience, plus a heavy dose of working-class Protestant work-ethic conditioning hidden in my DNA like a time-bomb.

As I embarked on my journey, my parents fell to arguing a lot about sex and money or both. I was drenched in their negative energies like an oil-soaked cormorant. I wanted to join the police and become a chief inspector and drive a flash police car. I wanted to join the army, wear a fancy uniform and win a medal. I wanted to join the navy and become captain of a battleship. I wanted to go back to being a child. I wanted to go back into the womb. I wanted to go home to the stars where I had come from.

As with all working-class children from that time, there were enormous pressures to find employment and to earn your keep. A whole mass of confused instructions. Don't get any big ideas. Do as you're told. Always wear a clean white shirt if you go to the doctor; remember he's not human, he's a god. Everyone is better, richer and higher up the social ladder than you are. Don't think, just do anything to earn money.

Conditioning cut in big time. I became confused and frightened and, in a panic of indecision, ended up working in the worst solicitor's office in the whole world as a humble dogsbody where I started to run my backside off for eleven pounds a week.

The boss was a disgusting drunk who slept most of the time on an old chaise-longue in his office, snoring like a pig and smelling of stale pipe tobacco and gin. He never did any work that I remember. The old dragon who ruled the typing pool was an insult to womanhood; she had a face like a hatchet, the personality of Vlad the Impaler and thin, spindly veiny legs. I don't think I've ever seen anyone so ugly in my whole life. Her hobby was making fun of people who were poor and who lived in council houses, because she had a detached house with gnomes in the garden and a forty-lever Chubb dead-lock on the door to keep out anyone she hated – and she hated everyone, including herself.

OK, all you New-Agers, I know this isn't exactly what you want. You want to read that everyone is a child of the Universe, and that I should send 'em all love and light, and that they can't help it because they don't know any better. You believe that they will evolve and send out love to the world one day and that they are just lost boys and girls really. Well, I'm sorry for being so negative, but it isn't necessarily so – these people were wicked by choice; they liked being that way.

Apart from that, I'm enjoying myself, so let me roll – it's better to burn out than fade away!

There was a junior clerk who did everything right. He pandered to his superiors relentlessly in the obvious hope that one day he would become a partner in the firm. The chief clerk was a crusty, prejudiced, nervous wreck and the other senior clerk was claustrophobic and cycled fifteen miles into work every day on an ancient bike with an acetylene lamp rather than travel in a car. When you went into his office you couldn't see him for pipe smoke. There was a one-armed articled clerk who was fifty years old and had failed his exams nine times, and another mousy sort of guy who handled all the money and was deep into the Order of Oddfellows. I once stapled his cacti together and he never forgave me. OK, they must have had positive qualities, but I don't feel like searching for them. I know I'm creating karma, but it's MY KARMA. My sins are my own.

All my hopes and dreams crashed. Fear of the future crept into my dreams and I could see no positivity or virtue anywhere. I wanted to go back, back to Mr Packer, but I couldn't, I was a 'grown-up' now. After deep contemplation and consultation with my higher self, I made the best logical solution. I became a drunk and a mod!

I was at Scarborough, I was at Brighton, dressed in my Carnaby Street military jacket and riding a gold-sprayed Lambretta SX200 motor scooter with four chrome mirrors, USA plates and two aerials festooned with tiger's tails, and a cherished picture of Diana Rigg as Mrs Emma Peel from The Avengers on the inside of the fairing. If none of this means anything to you, then look it up – English Social History of the Sixties.

The wild young warriors like myself grew weary of pop singers in sensible sweaters and of being patronised by Pete Murray and Alan Freeman. In came the Kinks and The Who, the Small Faces, the Rolling Stones, the Beatles, Cream, Pretty Things – and we all became absolutely 'solid gone' on our new-found freedom, off the wall WILD, and every moment of it was BLISS.

I didn't particularly hate rockers or greabos (people who rode motorbikes, for anyone who was on Mars during that period), as mods were supposed to do, because we were all really just the flip side of the same coin. The point was, it was a real rebellion against oppression and conformity. When we rode into a village on a Sunday afternoon, even the garden gnomes ran away and hid. Everyone said how awful we were, but if conventional society had approved of us we would have felt that we were being extremely straight and uncool.

I worked hard at drinking large amounts of Guinness, until I could consume ten pints a night and still ride the Lambretta. Of course, during the week I had to be a good boy at the office and wear a suit and be nice to people and know my place and touch my forelock, but come Friday night – Cowabunga!

Boys and men are essentially warriors, but there was and is no warrior expression, so we created it. The social commentators of the day thought we were mad, but then their idea of a good time was doing the small crossword in the local newspaper. The long winter evenings just flew by for them.

A rebel is simply someone who questions everything and doesn't accept hand-me-down beliefs; it isn't about hurting anyone, it's about being free, in all senses of the word. People told me there was a god 'up there' because the Bible said so, but then the Bible says that the first people were Adam and Eve and they had two sons, Cain and Abel. Cain kills Abel and goes off to the Land of Nod, east of Eden, where he finds for himself a wife – WHO? There were only three people left on the earth, so if the Bible is flawed in the first few pages, what other poisonous little lies are secreted in it? No way, José!

People told me there was a devil 'down there' but then, think about it. Consider the Holocaust and the Spanish

Inquisition. If there truly was a devil, could it really do a worse job than man had done throughout history? Isn't the 'devil' just a clever way of passing the buck? If the church placed an advertisement in a newspaper saying: 'Post of devil is now vacant, only really nasty pieces of work need apply', I think whoever got the job would look at history and say, 'Sorry, good buddies, I am a nasty piece of work but no way can I be more wicked than you've been, so I think I'll stay in the cosmic dole queue.'

Hymns are so boring and churches are so cold. The truth is far, far away from the messy fingers of people who like wielding power. Search for it. It is there.

I never 'did' drugs, mainly because I was too drunk on Guinness, but the era moved into the heady music of Pink Floyd and Led Zeppelin. The search for the Holy Grail was taking its toll and knights were falling by the wayside and getting picked off by the Mordreds of this world. All we ever wanted was to preserve the beautiful innocence of childhood in the big, confusing world.

I'm sure Jesus would have approved of us. He was a rebel too, after all. He only wanted people to be kind to each other and to have fun and dance and they couldn't even do that – so they nailed him up on a cross. So, in my Grail search I found myself virtually alone in the frozen wastes of my own dreams, running out of petrol, pierced through by arrows of condemnation and stabbed by daggers of poisoned words.

My sword was growing heavy, I'd dropped my shield miles back, dusk was falling and the road was going nowhere but I clung to my vision by the last red streaks of light on the horizon. Society had captured all of us, given us mortgages and lots of bills, sold us on the idea of being sensible, and even our pop heroes became sensible as they became richer. It was so sad, so many brave knights.

They loved us at Ypres and the Somme, Verdun and Gallipoli. There was a place for us there and on the Normandy beaches. But at that time there was no war and we were just nuisances so first of all they slowed us down, then they lobotomised us.

We were reduced to sitting on sofas watching Top of the Pops and fantasising. The Protestant work ethic took its toll and there was a fatalistic acceptance of conformity. The future seemed bleak. Acceptance was just a way of maintaining a clear mind in the face of so much confusion, so much bigotry and so much wrong thinking aimed at everyone as a means of distracting them and thus controlling them.

Live your life as a rebel, go to your grave defiant, touch the stars in the in-between time and be reborn as a warrior to light the world with truth, till all darkness has sped away. I never had and never will have any intention of going to my grave at all, but we'll deal with that subject later.

What with the conflict between wild living and conventional working, something had to give. Most people are born pure, then 'devils' sit on their shoulders and wear them down. Not just the devils of religious conditioning, but the devils of negative people's words; they weigh heavily, they give no hope, they offer no future, they destroy fun and pleasure. In my mind I crawled on looking for the grail, but I knew I was failing. Better men than I had tried; I was freezing now and there was no fire in my heart any more to bring on the thaw of inspiration.

Let's light a candle for every dream that has ever been dashed on the rocks of cruelty and for every tear that has ever been shed. A candle for every minute that good men and women have worked in vain to survive, for every good person who has been annihilated by a wicked lie and for every good-hearted soul who has ever been misrepresented. Then this world will glow in the firmament brighter than Sirius.

The whole Universe will see that we existed then – and they will see that here is a world of rebels, looking for the grail, looking for the truth, plagued by goblins that literally wasted people's time until they wasted away. It will be a prayer to the Universe to stop the goblins laughing, to drive them away forever, scatter them into the sea – assuming the sea will have them.

At the point of spiritual death, with Mordred almost triumphant, laughing his battle cry of 'You're no fun any more', came a voice of sheer perfect beauty via the television set late one evening on a show by a folk group called the Spinners. The voice belonged to Esther Ofarim, an Israeli singer (remember 'Cinderella Rockefella'?).

There was something otherworldly about it; it hinted that beauty and hope were not quite dead, and it lifted me up, captivated me. Oh, I know she wasn't the world's number one music star, she never aspired to the heady heights of Kate Bush or Madonna – they were front-line warriors, like Toyah Wilcox and Judie Tzuke and Joan Baez before them – but every dying knight has a different angel and Esther Ofarim's voice sang to me straight from heaven.

I had been fighting the system and the system had sucked me in, absorbed me. We empower whatever we engage in battle. Esther Ofarim's voice seemed to say, 'Come off the battlefield; people only die on battlefields, that's what battlefields are for. Regain your life, your hopes and your dreams in the mystery of woman.'

I found solace in buying every LP she ever recorded and listened to her voice almost continuously. It was like a healing balm and a benediction.

Shortly afterwards I formed a pen-friendship with a famous actress whose name I will never reveal. This lady became almost a guru to me, but I think I can say that I entertained her and she uplifted me and between her and Esther Ofarim I was finding the right road. I experienced a new dawn of understanding of the direction in which beauty and truth could be found.

Most of our perceptions of our realities are fantasies. We idolise a film or pop star and feel an affinity with them, as if they are a subtle part of our lives and as if they care about us. We touch wood to protect us from dark gods. We enact superstitious rituals, such as saying 'bless you' every time someone sneezes, all because, deep down, we need to believe that something exists that is stronger and wiser than ourselves.

This need passes if we attain an understanding of our own power and potential. We still have role models, but we admire them rather than feeling helpless. I started to pull myself together. The passage from the child world to the adult world had been painful and full of disillusion. Observations of people, spirits in transit who were not walking in the light, had saddened me. Looking back over my life thus far, I realised that I had learnt a lot and now I was starting to understand how to survive in the world of hard, dense matter, where good and bad fought it out with no quarter given or expected.

I had a strong body and a good mind and the knowledge that a woman was capable of liking me raised me up, even though she was distant, in the realms of fantasy. Her letters were real, she existed, she was no dream and she was suffering from the effects of goblins too, just as Mr Finch-Crisp had; and no doubt it was goblin energy that had created the thing in our first house. So now I had to learn how to fight in a more subtle and gentle way and I moved gradually into the realms of the feminine mystery.

The work in the solicitor's office became ever more pressured and I was becoming increasingly exhausted by it. A senior partner was brought in to assist the drunken boss. He came from Spain and didn't know anything about law (or so it seemed). He would give his files to me and tell me to sort them out by trial and error. (Ascended Master, he say: 'Select a solicitor with great care, select a doctor with even greater care, and select a guru with the absolute utmost care!')

One evening, while working late, I broke down in tears. I just couldn't cope any more. I was way behind with everything; there was no way that I could fit in all the appointments in court and work on the files and run all the errands and take all the flak that was coming at me from hatchet-face in the typing pool. She said she always hated me because I was somehow different. I used to think, 'Damned right, you bitch', but not that evening. The work had overwhelmed me and I just wept.

Moments later Jane, the receptionist, walked into my office. She was a nice girl and very pretty, although she tended to keep herself to herself. I immediately jumped up and, pretending to be riffling through some papers, turned my back to her as I was ashamed and embarrassed and didn't want her to see me in this state. I'd always had a secret liking for her and had often sensed her watching me. I felt that she understood my secret conflicts and inner struggles, but I had never dreamt that she liked me in any way.

She ignored my feeble attempts to hide my emotions and just came up behind me and put her arms around me, her head on my shoulder.

'It really isn't worth it,' she said fondly and softly. 'You see, they're all dead ... all of them. Oh, their hearts are beating, but whenever their hearts stop, there will be nothing left to carry on ... no love, no kindness, and no beauty. Let them go. You're not like them and never will be and you should never have tried to be like them in the first place.'

When I felt her sympathy and something sweeter than I'd ever felt before, I just broke down and sobbed. Esther Ofarim fed my spirit, but she was a recorded voice and it was the actress in her that fed my mind. Jane, however, was real. She was warm and solid and kind, but most of all ... she was there!

Words just tumbled out of me between sobs and convulsions of emotions, tattered tales of all I'd been through. All the battles and the insults, all the times of trying, all the fears, all the recriminations. She seemed to understand them all, as if she'd heard it all before.

'They hate you because you are kind,' she said. 'You show them up as the ugly spirits that they are. They don't know any better, literally. They don't know how to be kind. If you hate them, they will have succeeded in making you like themselves and will end up laughing in your face. I only have two words of true advice, which are, 'Be strong'. Look out of the window, come on – do it!'

I gazed plaintively through the window at the night sky.

'It's a full moon tonight,' she said, 'Look at the stars twinkling, and there's a cool breeze blowing. Come with me, we need to get out of here.'

She led me by the hand out of the office. I was too weakened by emotion to resist. Down the stairs we went into the fresh air of the street. Quickly she hurried me into the town centre and into the nearest pub. After a few minutes, she placed a double brandy in front of me and another in front of herself and, as we clinked glasses together, I managed the beginnings of a smile.

'It doesn't really matter,' she said. 'All that matters is that you learn from experiences, keep your health and, most of all, your sense of humour. Fancy a drive in the country?'

I shrugged, 'Why not?', still rather mixed up and embarrassed.

In a very short time we were in her car on the road north out of Swindon. Flat fields lay either side of the long, straight road, which seemed like an imposing strip of black tape stretched over a timeless landscape. The moon shone down over the wide horizon and I started to breathe easily again.

'That's better,' she said, as if reading my mind. "This is the real world. This land is as old as the sky – it's seen it all, and there's you worried about a crummy little office – let it go.'

As the car bounced along I gazed out of the window and my mind argued with my feelings. Half my mind said, 'Go to work, earn money, never give up, never cry, be a man'. The other half said, 'What a beautiful evening, stop thinking, just feel'. My mind seemed like a fractious child, constantly wanting attention until I finally managed to shut it up. It was then I couldn't help noticing the way Jane's skirt rode up further and further every time she pressed down on the pedals of the car, revealing more of her thighs with each movement, and suddenly my conditioned mind went to sleep and real feelings took over.

'See anything you like?' she said, smiling.

'Maybe,' I said, pretending to look the other way.

We pulled into the tourists' car park at Avebury and I was gently coaxed out into the cool evening air. Crossing a stile, we walked a little way across a field of long grass and resting sheep until we came to an avenue of stones with a wide deep ditch beside them.

'We are going to walk around the whole circle of stones,' she said. 'That's across the main road, right around and back to the field opposite the car park and in that time you will come to a very profound recognition.' She stroked one of the stones and strolled on, obviously delighting in the peace and quiet and energies of the night.

'And what might that be?' I asked, following her.

'Oh, do stop thinking,' she complained. 'It wouldn't be profound if I told you. It's no big deal, but just for once make a decision for yourself based on what YOU want, rather than what other people have told you to say and do.

'First of all you thought what your parents wanted you to think and that was your reality and your perception. Then you thought what your teachers wanted you to think and that became your reality. Now I would like you to think for yourself. Just ask yourself what you want. It's easy! Become wild, become a free spirit, join in the great game of life and have fun.'

I began to feel rather foolish, wandering around ancient stones at night with an attractive woman who seemed to know far more about life than I did. I tried desperately to think of clever impressive things to say, but nothing came so I lit a cigarette and pretended to be mystical.

We crossed the main road and climbed a steep bank, back on to the stone circle path again. A solitary car wove through the village and headed off to Devizes, lighting up the stones and fields for a moment.

The Universe shone down on me and a cool breeze caressed my face. The ground was soft and springy and strangely pleasant to the step, but it all seemed like a huge toyshop that I couldn't enter. I felt like an uninvited guest, a misfit and an oddity. I realised to my horror that

I'd never really had one true individual thought all my life. That I wasn't actually an individual! I was a composite figure of lots of people's thoughts and ideas all speaking through me and although they might have been good and kind and valuable, where was the voice of the real ME?

Jane had asked me, what did I want? And I guess I just wanted to be approved of, to get it right and for people to pat me on the head and say 'Well done, you're a really good guy'. It was at that moment that I realised I'd lost touch with the real world and had become part of an artificial system. I'd been tamed and rendered impotent!

'I want my innocence back,' I muttered finally.

'Which means?' she asked, stopping abruptly and leaning back rather provocatively against a huge standing stone.

'Which means changing, I guess,' I said, pondering deeply.

'In what way?' she asked, with the same penetrating stare.

There was a long silence. Sentences formed on my lips and receded through lack of air and then I took a deep breath and said loudly, 'I cannot go back to the office. I must leave it forever.'

'Oh, very good,' she said, smiling genuinely, 'that is what I wanted to hear. When I take you back to pick up your car, you must drive away and never look back. I have already typed out your letter of resignation. All you have to do is sign it and I will hand it in for you.' I was suddenly overcome by a feeling of panic.

'But what will I do?' I blustered. 'How will I earn a living, how will I pay my bills, how will I survive?'

'Just trust,' she answered. 'Trust in yourself and all this.' She waved her hands over the face of the sky. 'It will look after you. You have a destiny to fulfil; now you must go and begin living it.'

'But what about you'? I asked, genuinely concerned for her.

'You mustn't fall in love with everyone who is nice to you,' she answered, picking up on the note of urgency in my voice. 'I will either get married to some nice steady guy, have two children, a crippling mortgage and pretend that I never had any wild dreams at all, or I'll run for it – see where the winds of destiny take me.' She gazed for a moment towards Silbury Hill to the west and laughed, 'Second star on the right and straight on till morning. Don't worry about me,' she added with a smile, 'I can feel the wind pushing me already! I just had to make sure you were safe. It was painful watching your own conditioning kill you day after day.'

'Thanks!' I said, still somewhat confused.

'No problem,' she said lightly, running off down the hill. 'See you back at the car park."

LET US TRAIN OUR MINDS

TO DESIRE WHAT THE SITUATION
DEMANDS

Seneca 4BC - AD65

# Chapter Four

## Lilith

I never saw Jane again after that night, though I often think of her. Three days after leaving the career of law, I was working on a building site, humping bricks and shovelling sand and cement in the fresh air with the sun shining on me, from dawn till dusk, seven days a week and loving every moment of it. I was free and I soon became very fit, strong and healthy. With my first week's wages, I paid out more in deductions than I had earned in a week at the solicitor's office, so I was rich as well!

A couple of years went by and I was still living with my parents. I'd always felt I was rather lazy in the Great University of Life and had needed a severe shock from time to time to force me to evolve and move on. I would advise anyone to leave home as soon as possible. Love and honour your parents by all means, but you've already taken up at least sixteen years of their lives and exhausted them. Don't prolong their agony. For your part, there are hundreds of parties and fun experiences and love affairs to be getting on with so get on with them. Just be sure always to remember Fathers' Days and Mothers' Days, your parents' birthdays and Christmas and any other days when you feel they might need you.

Although we may have had many lifetimes and our spiritual DNA gleaned from all those experiences may burn itself into the simple blank DNA of one lifetime –

which does nothing more than dictate our shape and the colour of our eyes – nevertheless the ancestors who formed that simple blank DNA still matter very much indeed. We should honour our ancestors and since we have ancestors from each lifetime, we are related to a great many people, so we might just as well honour everyone to be on the safe side.

If you don't, God will open his big book on the day that you die, look you up and down, shake his head wisely (naturally) and say, 'Sorry, you're a dirty sinner, you were born in sin, you have always wallowed around in sin, all you have ever done is sin. You are lower than the lowest dung beetle, you are not fit to roll a ball of camel dung the size of a marble around the Sinai Desert, you make me want to throw up, so I'm consigning you to hell ... no, not even purgatory and that's bad enough –all these freezing souls wandering around feeling sorry for themselves looking like they've won the lottery but lost the winning ticket. No way – it's hell for you – forever!'

Next thing you know there's this nasty thing with horns shoving a red-hot poker up your backside, not once, mind, but over and over again – for ever – and laughing, as well as calling you names, spitting at you and leering, and when you look up all the angels will be sipping mineral water and sneering at you like little schoolgirls saying, 'Told you so, naughty, naughty, naughty! Now you're really sorry, aren't you?'

I'm sorry, I just had to get that out of my system – but be very sure you don't believe any of it!

Without any warning, at the age of twenty-two, I started to feel strangely disturbed. The feeling reminded me very much of the time when I was a child doing battle with the 'thing' in our previous house, yet it was a different feeling – not of impending evil, but of something coming into my life, something very powerful, and I became nervous and quiet because I could not explain the feeling away. I visited my doctor and took a few days off work to rest, but the feeling grew in intensity and then the pain started.

It was a piercing sting of a pain in the right side of my face. One moment it felt like toothache, then earache, then it was somewhere in the cheekbone and each day it grew worse and worse. I started to find it hard to eat and then to sleep. I took so much time off from work that I had to leave and began to look and feel really ill.

Doctors, dentists and specialists all examined me but no-one could stop it. Nor could painkillers. In the latter stages, I found that large quantities of brandy, plus half a tube of teething gel and six strong painkillers could ease it slightly, but no more. I tried my best to behave normally, but that too became impossible. I took to my bed and suffered in silence.

Sometimes I would go through a very angry stage and hit the pillows or even the wall, but I soon learnt that only made it worse. It did become worse, until one day I was sitting on the edge of the bed, holding my head, rocking gently, when I became aware that I was in a strangely peaceful otherworldly state, like a half dream, and I knew I was leaving my body. The body had become too painful to live in any more; I was dying, but there was no pain.

I flowed into this beautiful feeling in a state of perfect peace and to my surprise I became aware of three women standing over me. I can't remember them clearly but one had long, black hair; another long, curly auburn hair; the third I hardly recall. They were dressed strangely in gowns or robes, old-fashioned dress, yet not from a period I could place in history.

One of them, the dark-haired one, said, 'He's had enough.'

I came back into my body with a crash. I felt heavy and frightened but the pain was gone. I tried to make it start again by pressing my face and jaw, but it had most definitely gone. Before I could shout with relief and excitement, however, I'd slumped back on to the bed and slipped into a deep sleep.

In the weeks that followed I left home and rented a small terraced house. It was a marvellous feeling to have my own front door, with my own keys, and to be able to do whatever I wanted. I spent many happy and contented days decorating and buying furniture and making the place my own. I managed to get a clerical job in a builders' merchants' office just to make ends meet and settled into a new phase of my life.

Then the dreams began.

One night I dreamt I was lying on a dusty four-poster bed in some old mansion house. The walls were draped in dusty and tattered tapestries and I was dressed in blue military-style trousers with a white stripe up the sides and an elegant white shirt. I knew somehow that I was alone in the place and I knew also that I was very, very tired.

Suddenly I noticed firelight flickering on the wall above my head and I wearily got out of bed to investigate. I walked along a passageway beside a white balcony with tapestries to my right, until I came to a small window that overlooked the wide lawns which spread away from the house towards a high-railed fence and an ornate gate in the distance. (Why I didn't simply walk to the bedroom window and look out I'll never know, but then dreams follow their own rules and have their own logic).

There was a huge brazier, full of fire, in the middle of the lawn and a woman was tending the flames by throwing papers into the blackened drum. She had her back to me, but I could see that she was short and slim, with pure white skin and long, jet-black hair which reached down to her waist. She was barefoot and was wearing a simple, long, close-fitting black gown. I watched fascinated as she fed the fire with wild, dance-like, sweeping movements and the sparks flew higher and higher as if in obedience to her wishes. Then she turned, stood as still as some ageless statue and I found myself held firmly in time and space by her coal-black, humorous, ageless eyes. She smiled and the dream abruptly ended.

The dream had burnt itself indelibly into my mind and I was still entranced by her expression and her gaze well into the following day. She was, after all, extremely beautiful. However, by the early evening I had decided that the dream, although very vivid, was probably the result of eating cheese and crackers the previous evening or of too much stress. It had been a very profound experience, but I decided it was just a dream and I filed it away with all my other dreams in the memory banks of my mind.

Fourteen days later I had another dream. It had the same 'feel' as the first one, a sensation that signalled, 'Something very special is happening, so pay close attention'. I was climbing a dangerous, rocky, mountain path beneath a starry sky and a full moon. The land around me was harsh and forbidding with no trees or foliage to break the severity and although it was night, the heat was oppressive, which made breathing difficult.

I climbed up until I came to a cave where, inside, the same woman as before was sitting cross-legged on a red rug staring at me. Lanterns hung from the cave walls, illuminating tapestries and treasures of every kind.

'It's been a long time,' she sighed, 'and the centuries have made you weak and stupid. You don't even remember me, do you?'

I shook my head. I certainly wanted to know her, but my memory failed to yield anything tangible.

'Once you guarded me in paradise in the days when this world had three moons. You carried a sword as sharp as my wits and you were strong. Now look at you. Full of fear and night terrors, scared of your own shadow. At least I haven't changed.'

The luminance of her white skin, contrasting with her black eyes and hair, made her incredibly beautiful.

'Why is this land so dry?' I asked.

'Because you have no water inside you,' she answered. 'The way you see me now is through screens of your own making. Your body is drying up, your soul is drying up, that's why you can't think straight and why you can't remember me. I'll tell you a great secret, although once you knew it. Water itself is the fountain of youth – drink of it, renew the flesh, renew the spirit.'

The dream ended and I awoke at four o' clock in the morning. My mouth was dry. I walked to the bathroom and drank from the tap and realised that it was true that I drank very little and was often tired and slightly confused. Had I not read somewhere that the human body is ninety-five per cent water? If that were so, considering the large amounts my body must use, it probably was true that I was drying up. How were my cells managing to regenerate at all, with no water? Was my negligence causing me to age?

I decided that was a side issue. The big problem was whether or not I was going insane. Logically this woman had to have her origins inside my mind or totally outside of my persona. If she came from inside, then she had to be a sexual projection or an anima figure or a powerful woman created by my lonely subconscious to protect me from the wicked world. If she existed totally outside of me, well, that was a possibility which frightened me intensely so, in a state of total confusion, I decided to investigate.

I wrote to various groups and knowledgeable people until I eventually began a correspondence with an exclusive order of nuns in Oxford. One nun in particular, a Sister Angela, seemed especially interested in my story and invited me to write back and recount both dreams in full detail. After some time I received a letter back from her stating, 'The woman you dream of is Lilith, the last of the matriarchal age warrior priestesses. She fought the emergence of men until being killed in a ferocious battle beside the Red Sea. Of course her spirit lives on and she can incarnate again at any moment of her choosing. She became known as the "Queen of Battles". She has no fear and represents the wildness of raw energy. She tends the fires of the world but does not care for them, meaning that she keeps her ways alive, waiting for the downfall of the patriarchal age. If she has come to you, and it appears that she has, then it can only be because she knows you. You need not fear her, but be wary of her power because she is different from modern women. Her energy is very pure and therefore more powerful. Men have not polluted her!'

The dreams continued to come at fourteen-day intervals and each one was a teaching of some kind. She had the ability to create dream scenarios at will and to set the scene for a particular exercise or lesson, which she could dismiss again with a snap of her fingers. In the next and third dream she created a circular lake with a straight path leading to a tiny island in the centre. On the island was a plinth, and on the plinth was a large white book. She was standing in front of me and everything around me seemed dark and misty, as obviously scenery was superfluous in this context.

'That book contains all the answers to all the questions that mankind has ever asked,' she said. 'Go, take it – put the world to rights with it.'

I did as I was told. I felt it was wise to do as she told me since I always felt that her spirit was pure cosmic fire and if it wasn't contained in a body, at least for the benefit of my perceptions, it would reach the stars like a vast pillar of passion and wild, uncontrollable energy.

I walked up to the book and opened it and there, as she had said, were all the cures for every disease, the origin of the Universe itself, all the secrets of life. In a great fit of excitement, I held the book close to me and hurried off, my desires creating projections as I went.

My first desire was to rush into a hospital and to ask to see the chief surgeon, who was an illusion, of course, but an illusion who nevertheless listened coldly as I related the contents of the book. The next thing I knew, two very nice but firm security guards had frog-marched me to the entrance and dumped me, still clutching the book, on the hospital steps. I created several more hospitals in my passion to heal the world but the same thing happened every time.

In the end, exhausted, tired and sad, I created a pub and walked into it, stood on a table and said in a weak, disillusioned voice, 'Does anyone want to know the cure for cancer?'

Illusionary people muttered 'sad case' and 'nutter' and gave me awkward, fearful, sideways glances before an illusionary policeman placed me outside. I then found myself back beside the lake, staring into the timeless eyes of Lilith.

'You can only instruct people when they are ready to listen and to see,' she said. 'Each person has his or her own reality, which to them is as real as solid rock. Before you can change anyone, he or she must first either want to be changed, or you must find a way into their reality and break down the barriers of their fears. Now put the book back and sleep.'

The dream ended and I woke up startled by the sound of the telephone ringing loudly in my ear. I reached out and grabbed the receiver and mumbled 'hello'. I could hear my mother's voice almost screaming at me down the phone in a torrent of fear-filled words. 'I had this weird dream,' she babbled, 'but it wasn't a dream. There was this strange woman at the end of the bed, with long, black hair and black eyes and white skin and she told me to back off from you or else, and that you were her son, not mine and ...'

I buried the receiver under the pillow and put my head in my hands. Lilith was definitely not a figment of my imagination!

In the months to come the dreams intensified and Lilith taught me all manner of things through dream scenarios. Maybe I knew it all already on a deep level, maybe I'd known it all before and she was just reminding me, but it certainly seemed new.

She taught me that all matter is one. That the same sacred energy that flows through me flows through everything. That there is no separation. She explained the laws of cause and effect, whereby whatever is put out into the Universe, good or bad, goes around and comes around as either a curse or a blessing.

She showed me that the fountain of youth was not a specific fountain in some mystical part of the world, but water itself. Then, in one special dream, she seemed to dance timelessly like some immortal firebird, mocking the intellectual values that my society had come to accept as truths. Driven by some primitive and passionate energy, she revealed the nine deadly venoms.

'Conquer them and you live forever, but beware!' she said with a wicked leer. 'Each one is indeed a venom, the worst kind of poison, and is very, very deadly.

'Man has created all these delightful poisons for himself,' she laughed, swirling around in my dream and throwing fire into the night sky. 'Man is extremely clever and has used his big brain to destroy himself. They cannot touch me, as I never believed in them. I don't even belong here. I am simply keeping the energy pot boiling until the human race heals itself and is able to heal the good earth, but these venoms are deadlier than any snakebite.

'Don't you remember any of them? Does anyone remember? Through a veil of centuries in which reason has vanished and perceptions have diminished, everyone is an intellectual – a mind on legs, a mass of thoughts, walking around believing their existence to be real. They have forgotten the truth. Ah, how sad. They go round and round on the wheel of fortune, being born, growing up and getting polluted by each other's breath, getting ill and, oops, ... dying ... and around and around they go again.

'Now is the time to get off the wheel, be wise, move on, become part of the dance of life. Before you can do that, though, you have to get past these nine deadly venoms – nine tests, nine gateways and nine stumbling blocks. You have to ingest them, understand them and transmute them. Are you ready? Of course not ... but, ready or not, here they come.'

She leaned towards me, looking beautiful and deadly at the same time. With every movement, fire flew from her fingers and lit up the night sky. She was pure energy, raw energy, integrated into a beautiful form, immortal and indestructible and indomitable.

The dream changed into a courtroom and she was a stern judge, resplendent in a wig and silky maroon gown behind a high wooden bench with only the brooding shadows for company. I was in a dock with spikes around the outside, and against one wall hung the shadow of a noose.

'The first deadly venom,' she said, with great pomp and authority, 'is KARMA.' She shouted the word so loudly that it hurt my ears, even in the dream. 'That means if you're a thief, a killer or a torturer, or a sadist who enjoys hurting people or animals, or any life form at all, if your negative energy can be found in any life form in the Universe, then we will know, because that energy will bear your DNA configuration which is unique to you, and that means there can be no escape, ever.

'That energy will surely find you when the life form is freed of your pollution, then you will have to pay, not just for the initial pollution, but for all the ripple effects, backwards and forwards through time, and that will hurt and sting and smart and you're not going to like it.

'For example,' and here she banged a gavel on the bench, the noise of which echoed all around the chamber, 'if you hit a man and steal his wallet, you have affected his wife, his children, his parents, his whole family and everyone he knows, in fact, even his children's children, and everyone they know in turn, and so the negative energy of the original incident goes on and on into the future, creating miserable and painful ripple effects, on and on it goes ... and when all that comes back, it sure is going to hurt.

'That's at least three lifetimes of suffering – simply to learn the value of life and not to do it again. No-one judges you, you judge yourself. It's only your own rotten energy coming back to you; it belongs to you, you can't give it to anyone else because it doesn't match with anyone else, understand?

'Once you can say that no life form in the entire universe carries any of your negative energies then you will have passed the first test. If you have the sneaking suspicion that you may not have passed, there is only one way you can avoid suffering complete misery in a future incarnation and that is to PUT THE BLOODY MESS RIGHT BEFORE THE BILL COMES IN!'

STAY AT HOME

IN YOUR MIND

DON'T RECITE

OTHER PEOPLE'S OPINIONS

I HATE QUOTATIONS

TELL ME WHAT YOU KNOW

Emerson

# Chapter Five

## *Things my Mother never told me*

I woke with a severe headache caused by the intensity of the dream, a pain that grew steadily worse as I started to think back to any time in my life when I could have put my negative energy into a person or an animal or even a tree. She had said 'life form', and hadn't I read somewhere that the Earth itself was a life form? One thing I was certain of was that Lilith did not play games. If she said something was so, then it was so, and this was just the beginning, the first deadly venom, so I dreaded to think of what manner of further treats might be in store for me in my dreams.

It was a hot July day. I drove to Avebury and sat with my back against one of the circle stones, watching the tourists come and go and the light wispy clouds floating across the sky like trailing feathers. Everything was dry and baking under a thunderously hot sun.

My mind chattered away, as worried minds do, until the siesta mood of the day overcame me and I dozed in the shade of the huge stone. All sounds receded and I began to feel peaceful. I noticed that my headache had gone and there was just the faint longing in my heart, which I imagine we all have from time to time, for something real and good and tangible to appear suddenly and enter my life. Lilith was very sweet in a terrifying sort of way, but it would be nicer if she could have come and sat down beside me like an ordinary girlfriend. I reasoned that the dimension in which she existed was certainly inaccessible to me, although my own of course was easily accessible to her whenever she wished to slip down the frequency ladder of evolution and 'slum it' in goblin city, which was where I seemed to live.

I wasn't aware that I'd ever hurt anyone or anything, at least not consciously, not with, as lawyers would term it, 'malice aforethought'. But then as a little boy I had done some pretty nasty things to insects, so if I was going to be puritanical about the whole thing, I wasn't exactly squeaky clean and it was nice to appreciate that all things mattered, however small, and that one was inextricably linked to the destiny of all life forms. That idea eased the deep inner loneliness that again I guessed we all had, after being brainwashed for centuries by religion into believing that we were totally separate from everything else.

The thought came to me that I could pray for any outstanding little debts (or big debts, for that matter) of karma to be paid back to me in one payment, so that's what I did. On a beautiful sunny day at Avebury, I asked the Universe to pay me back in full for any past wrongdoing. I drove home thinking, rather smugly, that if anything were to happen it would surely be something very insignificant, such as stubbing my toe, since I had doubtless been a very good person, not just in this lifetime but also in all previous incarnations. Such is the arrogance of ego.

In the evening after dinner I sprawled lazily on the hearth rug in front of the fire to watch television. The television set was white and very large and rested on a stand. Out of idle boredom at the poor film I was watching, I rested my foot against the stand and very gently began to rock the television set to and fro, no more than an inch one way and then the other. On top of the television was a wooden ornament, an elephant carved from ebony. Suddenly it toppled from the television set and fell all of two feet on to a thick carpet and astonishingly split into two pieces. One piece catapulted across the room and hit me square on my top lip, knocking me unconscious for a few seconds and shattering my two front teeth.

For a few minutes I was in a state of total panic. Blood gushed from my mouth like a fountain, up the white walls, all over the white carpet and all over the furniture. In desperation, in a complete frenzy of fear, I telephoned a neighbour and babbled some incoherent screaming message to him. He came rushing in and almost fainted at the sight of so much blood, then desperately summoned an ambulance, which promptly whisked me off to the hospital casualty unit. It took several hours to repair my lip and a painful month passed before a dentist could fit crowns where my two front teeth had been. I looked a mess for a long time and during that period I never dreamt of Lilith once, but as soon as the swelling on my mouth started to go down and I started to look almost human again ... the dreams returned.

She was sitting in the Early Learning Centre playing with wooden bricks. She looked up at me and grinned wickedly.

'Walked into a door, did we?' she observed sarcastically. 'Thought you'd get away with just stubbing your toe, did you? You sadistic bastard.'

I complained bitterly and pleaded total innocence, but she merely picked up a cuddly toy panda and sat down opposite me, rocking the thing like a baby.

'Who dropped worms into jars of vinegar, eh?' she went on. 'Vinegar is acetic acid and worms breathe through their skin – horrible way to go. Remember the delight you felt watching them jerk this way and that in their death throes, suffering unspeakable agony and terror? But then, they were just worms; worms don't matter, worms don't have feelings, or DO they? Of course they damn well do!' She pulled the panda towards herself in a gesture of mocking protective horror, as if I was the monster from the black lagoon come to destroy all cuddly toys.

'Don't take any notice of HIM, Pandy, we don't like HIM, do we?' she cooed. 'And,' she went on, getting into her stride, 'who kebabed hundreds of assorted insects on to lots and lots of darning needles and stuck them in the back garden like some sort of childish primitive totem display? And who had to kill his own cat to put it out of its misery? Oh yes, I know you accidentally ran over it while reversing your car, but if you had been more aware and hadn't been in such a hurry and in such a bad temper, you'd have given the poor thing a chance to get away.'

'And who carved his name into the paintwork of his uncle's brand new motorbike? Made him cry, that did, yes it did, Pandy, and there were a few children at school whom you bullied mercilessly, so don't give me this model pupil, teacher's pet rubbish, it doesn't wash with me. On the last day of school, when your mathematics teacher asked you for your work file to show to his superiors and said that you were probably the best boy to ask since you were so attentive and conscientious, what did you hand to him in panic? A file full of papers gleaned from a correspondence course, so what message do you think that gave to him? You're a useless teacher, so much so that I had to resort to outside help, but here's the file anyway, just to rub your nose in your own inadequacies. Absolutely mortified he was, and yet you go on and on about how wonderful your teachers were, but you didn't always treat them very well. No, you were a spoilt, selfish, manipulative little shit and a creep as well. Pandy thinks so too, don't you, Pandy?'

'Is that all?' I grumbled.

'Since you mention it, no, it isn't all. You didn't have many friends, but the one you did have you imprisoned in your "punishment hole" underneath the floorboards of the den, which your father had built for you, when you were playing "escape from Colditz" and you needed a prisoner, remember? He's still terrified of the dark and of enclosed spaces. And you told him that a witch was coming into the tent the night you camped out with him and he ran off terrified, tripped over a tree stump and broke his arm in two places. You never did tell the truth about that incident, did you?'

She sighed deeply and added, 'You always lied to save your own skin and you often blamed others for things you had done to wriggle out of difficult situations. It is recorded in your energy that you once paid a mentally backward boy three pence to sit on the school bully, until the bully nearly suffocated and then when the teachers caught up with you, you blamed the retarded boy. It was nothing to do with you, you said, he'd done it all by himself.'

'So I'm suddenly Adolf Hitler.'

'No, Adolf Hitler is spiritually dead. He has ceased to exist because there was no way he could ever have paid off his karma, he'd have needed at least a thousand lifetimes in total agony and the Universe hasn't got the patience for time-wasters like that so it's as if he never existed at all, a chilling thought. I mean, never ever getting another chance, think about it.'

'What about my mouth?' I asked.

'Be grateful it wasn't your head,' she sneered. 'You got off very lightly, considering.' Then she started to parody me. 'Oh look, it's beautiful spiritual Avebury and what a lovely day it is and, oh gosh, I'd better check to find out if I have any karma due, so I'll ask for it all to be taken away. Well it has been, so shut up. And another thing, I haven't had sex in two thousand of your years and if I do it will be with someone more experienced and sensual and evolved than you, so don't expect me to magically appear beside you under the shade of a stone like some plaything. I ain't no plaything, honey chile, I am a complete universal bitch, always have been, always will be, got it?'

'Has anyone ever disciplined you?' I asked, feeling for once rather full of myself.

'Now I like that statement very much,' she said, smiling. 'It shows promise. I think I detect in you the first, faint, embryonic beginnings of what might loosely be termed courage, well done!'

'Why are you in the Early Learning Centre?' I asked.

'Why shouldn't I be? That is what this dream is all about, early learning – and to tell you all about the second deadly venom. Sorry you had to wait so long, but it obviously took you a while to get over the first one.'

'Oh God,' I groaned.

'No, God won't help; you see, if you put all the sacred energy together from every life form in the Universe – and that's a lot of life forms, believe me – that is what we call "God". You really ought to choose your words with more care, you know.'

'So what is it, then?' I asked.

She placed the panda back on a shelf and started to prowl around me.

'Look,' she said, 'about once in every millennium I choose to impart my great wisdom and knowledge to some lucky person. I am very special and I am very powerful and what I say is very special and very powerful so you'd better wise up and show some respect otherwise I'll dump you back in goblin city and forget that I ever knew you.'

'OK, I'm sorry,' I said reluctantly. She simply glared at me.

She picked out a plastic figure of a man and placed it on a child's table, followed by the figure of a woman and then a child.

'The second deadly venom,' she said slowly, 'is PARENTAL GENETICS.'

I looked at her in ignorance and she gave me a scornful look at my stupidity.

'How many times,' she went on, 'does a Hindu child become a Christian? Or a Christian child become a Moslem? Or a Sikh child become a Buddhist? Not that I have any time for religions but the analogy will suffice, and the answer of course is, hardly ever, if at all, because we have two DNA configurations. The first is what I call the 'blank' DNA. It contains instructions gleaned from the chosen parents of this particular chosen incarnation and when the spirit enters the foetus, which can happen any time from five minutes after conception to five minutes before birth, the spiritual DNA, carrying the experiences of many lifetimes, burns itself into the blank DNA to form the individual, but the blank DNA still has power. On top of that, in the child's formative years, it will learn only from the adults around it and will of course learn only what they are able to impart and, although it is all very well-meaning, it is mostly of no value.'

'But how does that kill you?' I asked.

'If both your parents believe that they will grow old and die around the age of seventy and if their parents in turn believed that, and if their grandparents believed that also – and so on, all the way back down the ancestral trail – then that is what they will teach you. Because you want to be approved of by your parents, you will believe it too and you will die.'

'So you're saying that our parents kill us?'

'Oh, they don't mean to of course, but because they believe in age and death, those beliefs are encoded in their DNA and they will pass those DNA codings on to you. These are the 'time clocks' that scientists are convinced exist to bring about decay. The second test is to break down the parental DNA from your own cellular system.'

'And how does one achieve that? It seems impossible.'

'While honouring your parents for creating the gateway through which you entered this particular incarnation, you must now abandon them. The Universe, with its trillions upon trillions of stars, must become your mother, your Great Mother, and the same Universe must become your father.

'You must become a child of the Universe, and you must not allow yourself to entertain any thought, belief or doctrine that your parents believed, except, if it is there – and it usually is – the vague notion that to do good is better than to do harm. Everything else is dangerous, everything else is a deadly venom.'

'But I have a duty to them!' I complained.

'What is duty but a debt to be paid back? Do flowers owe a duty to the rain for feeding them and to the sun for making them grow? Do they think that way? No, your parents are all mind, you must be no mind and all feeling and all knowing, totally aware.

'Your parents gave you entry into this life. The Universe gave you permission to enter existence itself. The Universe is your only true parent.'

'But I love my parents,' I said. 'This feels all wrong.'

She shrugged. 'I know it feels wrong – because your parents live inside you still and their parents and their parents before them. They all live inside you, that's why you feel disloyal, that's why you feel wrong. Only one problem', she said, lapsing into a Deep South American accent, ' ... they all dead.'

'My parents aren't dead.'

'Do they look old?'

'Yes.'

'Then they will die.'

'Well, I'll save them then.' I was feeling very upset now.

'And how you gonna do that, boy? Iron out their wrinkles? Wind the clock back? How you gonna save them?'

'I don't know, but I might just figure it out.'

'Well, you'd better be quick about it, otherwise you'll be too old and wrinkled yourself to even try. You'll be all tired and worn out with life. They live inside you, remember? You're just scared, it's not them you want to save, it's yourself, but you don't know how, just like they never knew – 'cos they all dead, boy!'

'They represent the only home I ever knew in this life,' I said. 'I don't think I could face the awful isolation of breaking free.'

'Oh, I know,' she said with a sarcastic note. 'All the sentimental images come swimming back, "mum" as the eternal solution to all problems and big strong dad who can keep the monsters away. It's all so cosy and quaint, just like sucking your thumb or clutching a teddy bear or being breast-fed. To be fair to you, most people never move out of this stage; spiritual babies I call them. Always looking to be parented and molly-coddled.

'They think that they are thinking, but in reality all they're doing is repeating the encoded reactive thoughts of their ancestors. Anyway, I'm bored with this place now, so what's it going to be? Are you going to move on through the Universe and grow up or are you going to stay here and look for someone to mother you?'

'Well, I suppose I'd better move on,' I said rather pathetically.

'Well, don't get too excited, will you!' she snapped. 'Let's not get too over enthusiastic here. I'm only trying to prevent you from getting old and wrinkly and forgetful. I would call that a pretty nice gift myself. Now repeat after me ...'

I sat up straight and tried to look profound and serious.

'I of unknown name, unknown origin and indeterminable age' ... I spoke the words a little too weakly for her taste.

'With gusto,' she commanded, 'as if you're celebrating your release from a dungeon!'

I tried again and apparently got it right that time.

'Release myself from this and all ancestral trails.' She paused for me to speak the words.

'Reject all parental and ancestral teachings, save those that are in total accord with universal teachings.'

She paused again. 'And I declare myself to be a totally free child of the Universe.'

'There,' she added, when I'd finished. 'I want you to repeat that over in your mind at least fifty times each day. Write it down on bits of paper and stick them up everywhere; beside your bed, on the bathroom mirror, wherever, so that they burn into your weak and fear-filled brain.'

When I awoke I drove to Avebury again. It was Sunday, so I had the day off to think about all that had happened. I sat down again with my back against my favourite standing stone. I could feel the awful pain of imminent separation as my parents and ancestors pulled away from me, leaving me alone and seemingly helpless in a vast universe.

At the same time, there was a heady feeling of joy and elation, as if I was following my heart, my hopes and my dreams for the very first time. I had to leave them behind, but it was sad to say goodbye. Thank you and goodbye. The cool breeze blew lightly on my face, tossed a few seedling grasses around as if tugging my sleeve and urging me to leave now. High above me a swift circled lazily and called to its mate. I felt like a traitor and a hero, an outcast and a warrior, when suddenly I felt my spirit break free and I was at one with all life as my body moved to a different, deeper, more passionate rhythm.

I didn't dream of Lilith for several weeks. It was mid-September and the days were growing shorter. The weather was still hot, but already one could feel the wild winds of autumn rehearsing in the chiller evenings ready to wreak havoc with the sonorous dreams of summer. I missed Lilith. OK, she confused me and made me feel inadequate and insignificant sometimes with her jokes and peculiar way of teaching and sometimes she frightened me with her power, but she was very attractive and I knew that she was only being hard with me in order to make me stronger.

I realised that I was very fortunate that she related to me at all. Often I would wonder where she actually lived and how she actually lived, what she did in a normal day and what sort of friends she had, on her own level of understanding. Then I would smile at the vast gulf between us, the vast gulf of evolution and understanding; or maybe, I reasoned, the gulf was not as wide as I imagined – it was simply that she had far less fear than I did, and therefore much more perception.

Everyone I knew, including myself, was suffering from SAD, long before 'seasonal affective disorder' was thought about, when it was just called 'the being-cheesed-off-with-the-thought-that-the-beautiful-hot-weather-was-slipping-away-and-soon-it-would-be-cold-and-wet disorder'.

It was on the last night of September that I finally dreamt of Lilith again. She was dressed as a schoolgirl, in a gymslip and black patent leather shoes.

'Where the hell have you been?' I asked.

She made a gesture of exasperation. 'You keep getting your choice of words all wrong,' she snapped. 'There is no hell. The term 'hell' is a patriarchal priesthood invention designed to frighten people into submission to church law and establishment dictates. It doesn't actually exist, although I hear Bangkok is getting very close, but to answer your question, mummy said I wasn't to come out to play after dark.'

'You haven't got a "mummy",' I scoffed.

'I did have too, once, a long time ago, and she said that if I went out to play after dark, especially on my own, then some nasty man was sure to whisk me off in his car and play with my naughty bits, that's if I was lucky. If I wasn't so lucky he would kill me and eat me, after playing with my naughty bits first, of course, 'cos everyone is obsessed with naughty bits.'

'I see.'

'No, you don't, you don't see at all. You look at things, but you don't see them, you listen to things but you don't actually hear them, and you touch things but don't feel them, just like everyone else. I couldn't come in the day, your day, that is, firstly because you wouldn't be asleep and I would sure as hell freak you out if I appeared beside you while you were eating your baked beans on toast. Wow, you sure know how to spoil yourself; the long winter evenings just fly by for you, don't they!

'Secondly, because daddy said that if I went out in the day I would probably get run over and splattered all over the road by a big nasty bus or lorry, or I would catch a cold since the weather, your weather, that is, has been a bit cold of late. Or I might get lost and never find my way home, and then I'd wander around getting more and more scared until night fell and then someone would come along and do naughty things to me, or kill me, or sell me to white slavers.' Then she grinned sweetly at me.

'I'm not to talk to strange men – and you're strange!'

'This is all nonsense,' I scoffed. 'You are not a helpless child, you are very powerful and very mean.'

'Oh, no, no. Daddy said I wasn't to have any big ideas like that. He said I should know my place and be happy with what I had and to do everything that I was told or else.'

'Or else what?'

'Or else he'd beat me, of course. That's what grown-ups always do, isn't it? Did you know that you only use five per cent of your brain?'

'No, I didn't.'

'Sad, isn't it? Want to know how much I use?'

'No, but I guess you're going to tell me.'

'Fifty-eight to fifty-nine on a good day, my days, of course, which are different from your days. You exist in a different time frame. That means that ninety-five per cent of your brain is fear and only forty-one per cent of mine is fear. Evolution isn't measured by academic intelligence, you know, but rather by the amount of fear one has overcome.'

'Why are you dressed as a schoolgirl?'

'Why, don't you like it, you lecherous old molester, you? Mummy and daddy warned me of men like you. You hide behind bushes in dirty raincoats and you read dirty magazines and you steal things and you smell and you beat people up. You're always getting lecherous thoughts about me, which you pass off as "romantic". I thought you'd like it. My mummy said that people like you take drugs as well, and drink and drive.'

She sighed. 'I'm dressed as a schoolgirl because then I can go to school and fit in with everyone else and learn all the things that mummy and daddy want me to learn, 'cos if I don't I'll just stay thick and then no-one will ever marry me and I'll never get any decent opportunities in life so I'll never have a really good career with a very high salary, assuming that I choose to have a career, before I'm lucky enough to get married, that is – and I'll end up with no money, poverty-stricken, alone and destitute and have to dress in rags, and probably beg in the streets, or survive by visiting soup kitchens.'

'Will you please shut up?' I said.

'And everyone will look down on me and say, "Oh look, there goes that thick scruffy girl who never listened to what she was told, who never behaved herself.'

'Shut up, please ...'

'And I would die alone of hypothermia in the poorhouse, collapsed over a bowl of soggy porridge.'

'SHUT UP!'

'Very well. I'm supposed to do whatever grown-ups tell me, after all – except for getting into cars with strange men, of course.'

There was a long silence. She folded her arms, pretended to ignore me and looked away, with her nose in the air.

'What has all this got to do with the third deadly venom?' I asked.

'Everything,' she answered stiffly. 'That's exactly what I've been talking about, except you haven't got the basic intelligence to work it out. You completely missed the whole point didn't you? Can't you try and think in a more lateral way?"

'The third deadly venom,' she went on with great pomp, 'is ... CHILDHOOD CONDITIONING.

'Tomorrow, when you wake up in your world, I want you to buy yourself a large notebook and make three columns on each page. In the first column I want you to list everything that your parents ever taught you – and I do mean EVERYTHING. Not just your parents either, but any other close relatives who influenced your early development.

'This will take you a long time and I want you see it as homework. Everything from "Don't walk under a ladder, it'll bring you bad luck" to "Suffering is good for the soul". Then, when you've finished that, write in the second column "yes" or "no", depending on whether you believe that statement to be true, and in the third column, next to any subject for which you have written "no", write down what you perceive to be the truth, and I'll see you after Christmas.'

'After Christmas!' I protested.

''Fraid so,' she shrugged. 'This will take you a long time. Everything has to be examined and unlearnt.'

'Do you have Christmas on ... er ... your world?' I asked.

'Of course not. The Nazarene did not incarnate on my world, so we have no need for a Christmas. Anyway, it's like Christmas all the time where I live because we're not so afraid of losing out all the time as you are, therefore we are able to give much more to each other. I don't think there's been an incidence of poverty or even a mild case of loss on my world for over 200,000 years, our years, of course, and they're much longer than yours.'

I pondered all this for a moment, feeling a headache coming on.

'I ... live ... on ... a ... different ... planet,' she said slowly, talking like a half-wit for my benefit. 'Goodbye ...'

'Why are your years longer than mine?' I called out to her, and as her voiced faded away into the distance, she answered, 'Because our sun-star is bigger, therefore my planet can be farther away and the orbit is longer ... Get on with your homework. You'll be in deep trouble if I come back and it isn't finished.'

And so she left me for a while and with a heavy heart I realised that escaping deadly venoms and moving onwards and upwards through the Universe was, in reality, very hard work.

THERE IS PERHAPS NOTHING

SO BAD AND SO DANGEROUS

IN LIFE AS FEAR

Jawaharlal Nehru

# Chapter Six

## *Who's afraid of the big bad wolf?*

Over the next few months, I filled three thick notebooks with 'things my parents have taught me'. The more I listed, the more I discovered and the task was seemingly endless. I kept recalling more and more incidents, last thing at night or first thing in the morning or while strolling into town, and I'd scribble them down in a smaller notebook to be added to the main list later.

I realised that I thought 'God' not only existed but that he was a white English Conservative as well. Foreigners could not be trusted. We have only one life. There is no meaning to life, just grab whatever you can and make the best of things. You will grow old and die. If you pass someone else on the stairs you will have bad luck. If you see a solitary magpie then you will lose your partner. Walking under a ladder, looking at the full moon behind glass, the number thirteen, spilling salt, shoes on the table, any dark bird circling over the house, all of these bring bad luck. If you go out in the cold and the wet you will catch a cold, or worse. Stick with the things you know, they are safer. On and on the list went, covering every aspect of life, until often I thought my head would start spinning. I eventually finished it on 19th of December.

Two whole days had gone by without any new additions to the list. Going through it and writing 'yes' or 'no' in the second column was relatively easy. I agreed with only five things on the whole list. It doesn't matter now what they were; what did matter was the startling revelation that ninety-nine point nine per cent of all the things I'd ever been taught were wrong.

Because I loved my parents, this notion caused much guilt and inner turmoil. Writing down the truth about each item was quite difficult, because most of the time I didn't know the correct answer. I figured I would come to know this one day, so I just placed a question-mark next to those items.

Against other items I simply wrote the truth of my feelings. For example, I did not believe it was necessary to say 'bless you' to people when they sneezed because I didn't believe they were likely to be suffering from the first symptom of bubonic plague (which is how the custom came into being).

The aspect of this exercise that horrified me most of all was realising how little original thought I actually possessed. My parents had passed everything, from their understanding of mundane living to their concepts of higher philosophy, on to me. I'd hardly thought about anything for myself. I realised, too, that when I encountered a new situation in my life I invariably used my parents' dictates to deal with that situation or to evaluate it, which made my thinking very predictable. So predictable, in fact, that I would most likely deal with any situation in exactly the same way as my parents, following the same logical routes based on the same dictates. The only difference was the practical circumstances surrounding me – for example, I had a car and they didn't.

In the first column of my homework I'd written 'I believe illness to be caused by random chance, bad luck, a bit like a lottery'. In the second column I'd written 'no'.

I couldn't accept this, it made no sense, so in the third column I wrote, 'Illness or dis-ease is the manifestation of a causal energy, placed in one's body by another person or by a situation created by another person'.

Likewise I'd written, 'Time is a fact of life. It wears everything out. It destroys and decays everything and it slips away very fast. If I live to be seventy I will be very lucky.' Against this, too, I'd written 'no', because I worked out that even on a very mundane level of thinking we must have a great deal to understand about the subject. In the third column I wrote, 'Time is a name we give to motion. One revolution of the earth around our sun-star we call a year and one revolution of our earth on its axis we term a day. We divide these abstract distances up with all sorts of mechanical and digital devices, and I cannot see how motion would make me look older. Therefore there has to be another cause of visible human ageing, which I believe to be the nine deadly venoms'.

I'd written that death was a horrible, painful blackness, a terrifying thing that ended everything and made all thoughts and emotions irrelevant and pointless. There was nothing after death and even if there was, it would be the unspeakable horror of being able to feel all the pain and sadness of life without being able to change anything, or even to be seen or heard. That was a possibility, but it was more likely to be a total oblivion, a state of non-existence. I wrote 'no' to this statement mainly out of desperation, because if that's all there was, then life itself seemed pretty pointless.

The notion of death frightened me, right down to my DNA, which contained memories of other people dying horribly, slowly and being humiliated at the same time, stripped of all dignity, pride and honour. In the third column I wrote, 'Death occurs when the human body becomes so polluted by negative energy that it can no longer function.

'Since cells are continuously regenerating, there is no reason why the body cannot survive indefinitely, but negative energy lowers the rate of reproduction, the body cells can no longer keep up, cellular frequency drops and atomic weight rises, thus gravity exerts a greater pull upon all the vital bodily organs. Systems begin to fail and death occurs. However, assuming one has control over the absorption of negative energy and is able to transmute it, the body will stay attractive and vital until one chooses to die. Having learnt all that one came to learn in this particular incarnation and having done everything that one came to do, one could then go home to the stars.

'Death then would be a conscious "switching off". A beautiful thing, as easy as a cool breeze caressing one's face, but this will be hard to realise since one's DNA will probably have no record of such a way of dying, except maybe as a dim and distant dream–memory. Assuming also that the body was always young and vital because all deadly venoms were being dealt with and transmuted, one could keep this form, at various levels of vibrational frequency, and move between worlds and between dimensions at will'.

I have always refused to believe that the Universe is so sadistic and so cruel that it creates beautiful women and strong men and then day by day takes away their beauty and strength and eventually mocks them with senility. I could never accept the blind acceptance of this doctrine taught by theologians and philosophers.

It saddened me to see people who had once been beautiful, vital and strong now withered and feeble, and I knew there must be another cause. The cause was, I realised, that negative people, people who irresponsibly pollute all life forms with their negative energy, slowly kill other people, putting them first into hospitals, then into homes for old and discarded people and finally into cemeteries, and then they blame fate in order to escape retribution and justice.

Negative people will say that all things die. Not so. All things change – so a person can still learn and evolve and progress while remaining strong and beautiful and uncorrupted. Change is a positive constant in the Universe while death is an illusion created by tyrants in order to enslave people.

One could liken flesh to a river: the river flows and the water is clean, but if people throw their junk into the river, it silts up, stinks, becomes stagnant and then ceases to flow at all. Flesh functions in the same way. Universal energy must flow through it and negative people must not block the meridians with their mental and emotional junk; that way the body will remain clear and clean and healthy and beautiful.

Negative people are always messy and dirty, because mess and dirt create stagnation and decay, which gives off a negative energy in which they feel comfortable. They prefer to breathe negative air, and they will try to spread their mess beyond the confines of their own space into other people's spaces so that they have more territory in which to move.

If one negative family moves into a street, the positive neighbours are disgusted by the energies and move out, to be replaced by people who find negative energy comfortable. Thus the whole street becomes negative, then the district and eventually the whole town.

People need to be totally intolerant of others who are messy and dirty, whether the mess and the dirt are physical and visible or whether they are mental and invisible. Although they may be invisible, they can surely be felt as a deep gnawing ache in the pit of one's stomach and as a myriad of quasi-physical disorders.

It is strange how good people will not permit someone to tip garbage into their front gardens or to leave cigarette ends around in their cars, yet they permit their bodies to be polluted by other people's messy energies, the body being their most precious physical object.

Perhaps one day we will wear 'negative-energy detectors' on our shirts, which change colour when someone is polluting us, so that we can say, 'Hey – back off, keep your rubbish to yourself, you're damaging my cells, you're slowing down the rate of my cellular reproduction – you're making me look old and wrinkled – how dare you!'

As one's cellular frequency drops, so the body's atomic weight rises, thus allowing gravity to exert a greater and more damaging influence on the body. In fact, when exposed to negative energy, a person's weight increases, and if it were possible to wear a device that monitored physical weight, people would be amazed to see their weight increase by sometimes as much as a stone when in the company of a negative person.

Because people weigh themselves perhaps only twice a year they never notice this subtle change. But if one were a highly evolved being who could raise one's vibrational frequency far beyond normal human capabilities, eventually one's atomic weight would be the same or less than water. This is how Christ was able to walk on water.

The things that I'd written on my list about sex were incredible. I believed sex to be base, dirty, unpleasant, a dressed-up version of rape. In the second column I wrote, 'no' but in the third column I was lost for a truthful answer so I wrote, 'I don't know' although I knew at least that my original encoded ideas were wrong and that was a start.

The subject of sex seemed to arouse so many disturbing feelings, most of them based on vague, enigmatic ideas. It was attractive and desirable, yet wrong and dirty. It was needed, yet it was taboo. It was pleasurable but sinful. The sexual act was solely to produce children. God says so; the whole business is fraught with danger and always leads to misery. These were the deep-seated ideas, and I had no answer to them except to say that they were wrong.

I had been taught that it was good to be poor and it was good to suffer. Of course I wrote 'no' to both of these ideas on the grounds that a loving god would not wish me to struggle and hurt, so in the third column I wrote, 'It is not God or the force of the Universe that causes poverty and suffering, it is the negativity of a few human beings. As long as negativity is tolerated there will always be tyrants and people who seek to exploit others.

I believe that the Universe tries to change them gently, rather as Scrooge is changed in Charles Dickens's A Christmas Carol, but if they don't yield to reason, then they are forced to understand by having their own negative energies thrown back on to them.

I seemed to believe that I would always be poor, because I could never save enough after paying all my living costs to come even close to being rich. Again I wrote 'no' to this and answered, 'I will always be poor if I think that way. I need to open myself up to higher forms of thinking which embrace concepts such as abundance and the ability to receive.'

My conditioning had taught me that rich people were better than I was, because to be rich they would have to be successful and therefore had to be cleverer than I was. I wrote 'no', and answered, 'Some young spirits need material wealth to allow them to tackle the first of life's tests without the worry of paying their way in the practical world. Because they would not be able to handle the stress of doing so and therefore they wouldn't learn anything, they choose to be born into rich surroundings. This is a different concept from abundance; abundance is wealth with awareness.'

I had written, 'I must be extra nice to people who want to be with me, because I can't stand to be alone.' Certainly my parents were the source of the idea that I should be compliant towards anyone who was with me on the basis that they were doing me a favour by keeping me company, regardless of their motives.

The fear of being alone came from the fact that my parents were not always around, which wasn't their fault, of course, and this weakness, this need, obviously gave negative people great power over me. They could say, in effect, 'I'll give you company, eat all your food, smoke all your cigarettes, drink all your wine and use you on condition that you don't object and you do as I say, otherwise I'll leave you all alone and then you'll be sorry. Think of the small hours of the morning, the long, wet, dreary Sundays with no-one around, then you'll be sorry.' I answered to myself, 'I must learn to like myself enough to enjoy my own company; that way I can relate to positive people when I choose, and no-one negative can blackmail me with my own needs. If I learn to love myself enough not to need anyone, then I will be free to like and to love people as I choose and to appreciate relationships with them fully.

I'd been taught to believe that I had to have eight hours sleep a night or I would not be able to function, yet I knew that on occasions, when I'd been really happy with someone, I'd stayed up talking all night and hadn't been tired at all, so I realised that the amount of sleep one needs is proportional to the amount of fear one has.

The brain has to rest, and fear tires it out. I believed that unless I had breakfast in the morning and a large meal in the evening I'd become ill, when the truth is that the body needs water, since our bodies consist of 95% saline water. We need only relatively small quantities of highly nutritional food, yet the more fear one has, the more one eats, because it offers a feeling of security.

On the night of 23rd December Lilith came in my dreams again, looking very frightening indeed. She had assumed the form of a vampire wearing a long black cloak with a silk maroon lining and I could faintly see the hint of fangs glistening between her bright red lips.

'Hello,' I said, rather feebly. 'It's good to see you again.'

She didn't answer, just gave me a long, ice-cold look as if she was going to attack me.

'Stop playing games,' I said. 'Get on with whatever ... well, with whatever you've got to get on with.'

She grinned and the expression was so sinister that it terrified me. The dream became a nightmare. I struggled to wake and couldn't and found myself running in a blind panic through castles and forests and overgrown cemeteries, but always she was ahead of me, barring my way, leering at me.

'There is only one thing worse than a nightmare,' she hissed, 'and that's a nightmare from which you cannot wake. You are trapped in illusions, but I'm real.'

I ran away from her, thinking that my heart would burst. Down long dark corridors in strange mansions and wherever there was a shaft of moonlight, I could see horrible tapestries and paintings portraying long-dead sinister people, witch-burnings and other executions. Then I found myself in the middle of wild moorland. A wolf howled from out of the darkness and dark clouds scudded across the moon like clawing fingers – and always she was ahead of me.

By this time I was totally exhausted and could run no further and there she was, about twenty yards away and moving towards me very slowly. When she was close enough to touch me, she raised her cloak above her wings and attacked and, as her fangs sank into my neck, I saw a succession of images from my past.

I saw my mother nearly choking and me saving her. I saw myself floating out into the cold, rough sea on an airbed; the dark energy I'd seen as a child; an old silly 'B' movie with flying saucers sinking into the grass of a back garden; Quatermass and the Pit, being left alone and crying for someone to come home; being lost; being attacked and savaged by a huge black dog; even the dark despair of failing my 11-plus examination, which seemed at the time like the end of my life. Just as one sees brief cameos of people flash by in the carriages of an express train as one waits on a railway station platform, so I saw all these things and more. Then the stream of terrible memories ended and she was no longer a vampire. She was the Lilith that I knew and she was grinning at me and there was a hint of compassion in her smile.

'Scaredy-cat,' she said.

'Was that really necessary?' I asked pitifully.

'Oh, yes,' she answered. 'Welcome to the fourth deadly venom – FEAR. Oh and by the way, congratulations on your homework. I've given you thirteen per cent and before you complain, that's really good for someone who only uses five per cent of his brain. There wasn't much that you missed.'

'You didn't have to frighten the wits out of me,' I complained.

'Oh, but I did,' she went on. 'You see, most fear is suppressed, that's what makes it so dangerous. We're not even aware that it is there. We inherit a lot of it from being exposed to the fear energy of our parents. Some comes from early unpleasant observations, which carried with them unpleasant feelings, and the remainder comes from our spiritual DNA drawn from frightening incidents and observations in past lives.

'Fear and conditioning are very much intertwined. For example, you may not have acted out of fear in a conditioned behavioural pattern drawn from your parents, but your action was created by the fear of your parents and passed on to you as an idea, an aspect of life to which you then subscribe. Therefore fear is the worst dis-ease on this planet.

'People incarnate here to overcome it and then forget completely why they came here. The more fear a person has, the less perception he or she possesses, and the less perception, the less one learns about the realities of life and the Universe. Why are you so afraid of Christmas?'

'I'm not.'

'Yes you are. You're afraid of being alone at Christmas because you're scared that seeing your parents in your old home will bring back disturbing memories and feelings. You're afraid that, having spent so much on presents in an effort to please them, you won't have enough money after Christmas to pay your bills. Your parents lived from hand to mouth and had a crippling fear of receiving and of spoiling themselves and you in turn have a fear of destitution.' She smiled knowingly at me, a kindly smile for once.

'You dreaded Christmas, didn't you?'

'Yes.'

'Why?'

'Look. I love my parents and they looked after me very well. They always did their best and I am very grateful to them for that.'

'That doesn't answer my question.'

In my dream I began to cry and through my tears I managed to say, 'I'm really sorry that I'm not as smart as you. I'm really sorry that I don't use fifty per cent of my brain and I don't have all the answers to the Universe. I'm doing the best I can with what little I have so, please, if you can't stop rubbing my nose in it, just go away and leave me to limp through life with my pathetic five-per-cent brain.'

The dream ended and I woke up with tears still on my face. It was the morning of Christmas Eve. I went downstairs and threw a handful of final demand bills at the wall, looked in my wallet and found just one solitary ten-pound note. I cast my eyes around the house and it seemed so dull and tired. It was then that the realisation swept over me that I had nothing.

The house was rented; I lived from hand to mouth and I rarely saw anyone worthwhile. I didn't go anywhere or do anything worthwhile because I didn't have enough money. I had an old car that was illegal and falling to bits with rust, and there were just three Christmas cards on the dresser. Worst of all, I had no future that I could see. I slumped down on the couch, head in hands, in a violent fit of despair.

On impulse I drove to the icy fields of Avebury and cried, out of sight behind my favourite standing stone. Down and down my mood went until I was almost suicidal. Down and down, too, went the quality of my thinking until I hated myself and could no longer see any glimmer of hope or relief from the feeling of desolation.

The only comfort I could find was in the memory of Jane's words, when she had taken me to Avebury some time ago. 'Trust in yourself and in all this,' she had said. The sky was a steely grey and hinted of snow and the wild, chill wind gnawed at my face. I was alone with my own monsters. I began to walk, following the route I'd taken with Jane, until I crossed a narrow lane and climbed up a steep bank into a grove of leafless trees where I sat down on the gnarled roots and resumed my misery.

Suddenly I had a sensation of someone behind me. I turned quickly, but saw no-one. I was alone with the wind, the cold trees and the damp earth and the short murky day was slipping away fast. A strange, exhausted peace came over me as my mind spun with gloomy thoughts and images of what other people had and what I did not have and of how poor and unlucky I was and of how everyone would be enjoying themselves now, sitting beside cosy fires, in rooms with Christmas trees and decorations and presents and feasts waiting to be eaten and parties to be enjoyed ... until my mind became tired and eventually went blank.

All at once the trees seemed almost friendly. After all, they had no parties, they just watched the seasons come and go, as did the standing stones. I was almost too frightened to think anything at all because I knew that one sad thought would bring many others in its train, like one fish at the head of a whole shoal.

Then a thought came to me – a very profound thought, which wasn't sad. It almost burned itself into my brain and shocked me with its intensity. A New-Age person would say that it came from my higher self, a psychiatrist would say it came from my id, but I think it came from a helpful spirit who felt sorry for me, yet was wary of getting too close lest its high-frequency energy field become contaminated by my own low energies, which would cause it to nose-dive and maybe not recover.

The thought was: 'The only difference between seeing the landscape as beautiful and magical and mysterious and seeing it as sad and dull and forlorn, is simply what people have done to you'. I repeated it over in my mind several times and it was like a flash of lightning in a dark and forbidding sky.

Of course what I was seeing wasn't sad and forlorn, it was my mind that was sad and forlorn and the sadness wasn't even my own. It was the sadness energy of people who had gone before me and played a part in my ancestral evolution, the sadness of all their lost dreams and dead hopes. In a sense, I was carrying a cross for them and taking on their misery as a relay runner picks up a baton. The sins of the fathers are visited on the children (the word 'sin' correctly translated means 'that which is not well for you' – quite different from the usual meaning). What I had to do was raise myself up and help those who had gone before me, so that we could all break the chains of our conditioning.

Nature, when seen through sad eyes on a cold and wet day, appears to us as very dismal; conversely, when viewed through happy eyes on a bright and sunny day, it appears positively joyful. Therefore we create our own reality and credit inanimate objects with how we are feeling at any particular time. It was quite amusing to realise that if someone had been unpleasant to me during my first visit to Avebury, I'd probably always have associated the place with pain and sadness, yet if something blissfully happy had happened, then the place would ever have glowed in my mind. The only difference was in my mind and that difference was dictated ultimately by the way in which the energies of people had affected me in my life.

I could see clearly now why Lilith had emphasised the total re-creation of myself and the elimination of all flawed and negative inputs. Without her teachings I would inevitably colour everything with negativity and would project my feelings on to everyone and everything around me. But essentially those feelings were not real, neither were my observations and perceptions correct.

I drove home. I had discovered Zen, the eye of the hurricane of one's feelings where there is only peace, humour and serenity. I celebrated Christmas Eve in my own quiet way, resolving always to rid myself of negative programmings and replace them with truthful ones and to change all the practical things around me.

Anything that was drab or dull I would throw away. In future, I would surround myself with nothing but bright and colourful things. I would have candles and incense and beautiful music. I would make everything clean and sparkling and create a 'new me'. All my dull and play-safe clothes would have to go and in future I'd dress only in clothes that had style and quality. I resolved also to be much more spontaneous and adventurous.

Moreover, I would spoil myself, save money and be magnetic to my prosperity and abundance, until eventually I could buy my own house and a better car. In the meantime I would be grateful for all that I had, making sure, at the same time, that my surroundings fed and uplifted me and anyone else who came into my home.

At midnight on Christmas Eve, there was a huge bonfire blazing in my back garden. I was destroying the past and cleansing my surroundings. I scrubbed and polished everything in the house, made the rooms simple but light, airy and colourful. I worked hard till almost four in the morning, when I took a salt bath to cleanse myself from any residual negative energies and eventually collapsed into a fresh clean bed with crisp, sweet-smelling mattress sheet, pillows and quilt cover. The last dying flames of the bonfire created fascinating shadows on my bedroom wall and, feeling a great, new-found sense of achievement, I fell into a deep, beautiful sleep.

Some time in the night, the Spirit of Christmas passed across the Earth. I could feel it and sense it, even in my dreams. I had always believed, and I know that it comes every Christmas Eve from some far-distant world, in a galaxy billions of light-years away, sent by wise and benevolent beings to scatter the magic dust of kindness over the world, so that maybe we can do for one day what we seem unable to do at any other time – and that is to treat one another respectfully and honourably.

I believe that for a short time, this magic dust dispels fear of differences between people: fear of lack, fear of being undeserving, fear of losing, fear of being wrong, fear of being foolish and of not being liked or accepted, fear of being cast out of one's tribe or clan, fear that one's gifts will not be well received. Once a year, just for a short time, this magic touches people and they can know the joy of loving and of being loved in return.

If you listen very closely on the night of Christmas Eve and if your motives have always been truly loving and giving, you will hear bells, like fairy bells and, faintly in the darkness of the night, the sound of beautiful music and a deep sense of peace and beauty will come to you as the spirit of Christmas passes over the land. It is a truly wonderful time, and the next time children ask you, 'Is there really a Santa Claus?', you can truthfully answer 'yes', because in a sense there is and it is much more beautiful than you can ever imagine.

I always light a candle to this spirit, even though I do not know its name. All good energies love light and it has always felt right and proper to bid them welcome.

NEITHER A LOFTY DEGREE

OF INTELLIGENCE NOR

IMAGINATION NOR BOTH
TOGETHER

GO TO THE MAKING OF GENIUS

LOVE, LOVE, LOVE, THAT IS

THE SOUL OF GENIUS

Mozart

# Chapter Seven

## Beyond the Tower of Babel

In the early days of February, when the razzamatazz of Christmas was over and the bleary New Year celebrations had finished and the days had grown a little longer, Lilith decided to visit me again.

In the dream she was sitting at the top of a grassy hill, and I could see a bright crescent moon surrounded by countless stars with shadowy trees all around me that swayed gently in the soft night breeze. She looked at me deeply, staring right through to my very soul, but said not a word. I waited and continued to wait, until the curious and watchful moon had moved quite a distance from the point in the sky where I had first seen it.

I was feeling much better about myself now and the quality of my sleep was much improved. Therefore the essential me within the dreams was a lot stronger and more confident, so I just sat patiently and looked at her from time to time, as often as etiquette allowed, and waited. I realised that I was very lucky to have her relating to me, and I knew also that I would be thought of as mad if I tried to tell anyone about her, but that notion had ceased to matter ages ago. She mattered very much to me and I was prepared to wait, for ever if necessary.

I stretched out on the grass and thought, 'OK, if she doesn't want to talk, I'll send her some energy.' I gazed up at the stars, tried to link into them and to pass the energy on to her as a gift.

She closed her eyes and began to sway lightly from side to side. At first only her head moved so that her black hair fell around and over her shoulders. Then her whole upper body started to sway, so I tried harder, and the harder I tried the more she moved, until her movements were wild and chaotic but also strangely erotic and compulsive.

I refused to allow my mind to enter into it. No mind, no ego, no desire and no thoughts. I just continued feeling and willing energy into her, pure energy from the stars. Not my own energy, but pure Universal energy. I didn't know exactly what I was doing, but I knew it was good. Finally she placed her hands over her face and sighed and then sprawled out on the grass, apparently exhausted. Then she suddenly sat up and grinned at me, her head cocked to one side.

A beautiful wave of energy hit me, so strongly that I fell over and rolled some way down the hillside, but even as I did, I felt amazing. I felt as if I could almost touch the stars and understand them. I felt at one with the trees and the earth and all life; indestructible, immortal and complete, but most of all, I felt loved. Gradually the feeling melted into the good earth, leaving me smiling but happy, kneeling up on all fours and grinning back at her.

Instinctively I sat upright and began breathing deeply and focusing on the clean and pure energy of the stars. When I felt empowered enough, I sent the energy back to her, as a gift, a blessing and a benediction. She swayed wildly backwards from her sitting position, almost toppled over and managed to right herself. Her hair fell over her face and she began to breathe heavily and blow strands of jet-black hair away from her mouth; then she made a parting in her hair with her fingers, revealing her face, and looked at me, slightly humorously.

She stood up and took off her jacket, revealing a tight black top. Then, throwing the jacket away, she took a very deep breath, raised her hands to the stars, pointed at me with the forefinger of her right hand and blew. I felt as if a hurricane had lifted me off my feet and high up into the night sky, carrying me along for what seemed an eternity, until I landed with a soft thud on a steep, grassy bank beside a motorway, with cars and lorries streaming along in all lanes and in both directions.

There was a huge signpost just ahead of me that read 'London 25 miles' and I began to panic. The noise of traffic hurt my ears and the seemingly endless streams of headlights dazzled me. I don't know how I knew, but I felt certain that I was now hundreds of miles away from where I had been!

I was lost, confused and very frightened. It suddenly occurred to me that this was some sort of test and I found myself thinking, 'You are where you are inside yourself, you are where you wish to be and where you ought to be, not where you're told you are or told to be. Your essence is within, not without, and everything in the Universe is in its rightful place.' I began to relax and breathe freely again and, almost instantly, found myself back on the hilltop facing her. She looked very surprised to see me!

She clasped her hands together and placed them against her cheek in a gesture of sleep and the dream ended and I slept, at one with the night.

In the days that followed I became more conscious of the way most people never actually said anything real or true and were never really completely honest, either with themselves or others. All their speech and conversations were filtered through a sieve of protocol and fear and double meanings.

I had been aware of this as a child and always fancifully imagined that a man came down the streets in the early hours of each morning with a shovel, a handcart and a broom to sweep and gather up all the letters of all the words that people had spoken but never meant. His barrow was full of all the letters of the alphabet, with sometimes a few letters from foreign alphabets mixed in, and every morning there was a new load to be swept up and carted away.

I became painfully aware of just how inadequate language was and realised that music and paintings and all forms of art, in fact, were attempts to communicate and relate in a much higher language, the language of feelings.

I developed a deep dislike of intellectual thought for I realised that intellectuals 'talked' about love but never gave or received love and they talked about compassion and forgiveness and ways of being benevolent but never actually practised any of these virtues. It was all words, clever words, but words without substance. I realised that a trained parrot could say, 'I love you'. Many people were tricked by words, mistaking them for actions.

It was obvious that wise people spoke hardly at all, and when they did, each word was carefully chosen and had meaning and precise impact to create a correct image of feeling and a good outcome, whereas people who knew hardly anything about life simply babbled away endlessly or wallowed in negative reports of all aspects of life.

The lies of politicians irritated me, as did the way in which lawyers twisted people's words to mean whatever they wished, in their efforts to show honest people to be liars and dishonest people to be speakers of the truth. I also noticed how people, when angry, chose harsh words which shot into other people like deadly, poisoned arrows. Everyone seemed to be lying, and it amused me to think that in France people lied in the French language and in Italy people lied in Italian, and so on.

The world was being exposed to the energy of pointless babble in hundreds of different languages, when the real language of the world was feelings. I felt guilty of arrogance and of being judgmental but, all the same, I knew that I was learning something important, although I wasn't exactly sure what it was.

Lilith certainly didn't speak English to her friends and loved ones, indeed it would be arrogant to assume she might. Maybe she didn't speak at all, having evolved beyond the need for words and communicating solely with feelings, and maybe she spoke to me verbally only for the sake of ease of communication with what, to her, would be a lesser being.

I suddenly realised how hemmed in I was by ignorance and how limited I was in my scope of communication. Everyone in the world was trying to express the true language of feelings through words, because words had been taught to them and burned into their brains from birth, but the beauty of these feelings could hardly be conveyed at all. Where feelings are not communicated, there is frustration and fear, which leads to conflict. Thus the races of the world have been fighting one another for centuries, fighting to be understood correctly, fighting to have their feelings acknowledged.

I realised a fundamental truth, that the English language did not contain enough words, phrases or information to save me from growing old, becoming sick and dying. It simply wasn't comprehensive or deep enough. Neither was French or Russian or indeed any other language. The truth lay elsewhere; in the language of feelings correctly expressed. Then I understood why Lilith had come to me in the last dream without speaking

– she had been testing me to see if I could understand the latest test, the fifth venom, for myself and I had done so. It was LANGUAGE.

In the dream I had communicated with her with the energy of feelings and she had done the same, only more powerfully. I had been expressing fondness without words and she had reciprocated. We had been communicating the purity of our feelings in a way that was light-years away from speech.

When I thought further I saw that the first form of communication is violence. You attack and hurt and take what you want from someone weaker, with fists, weapons or a threatening attitude. The second form is words, but how often are words used correctly and kindly? Most words are used to take and to steal through manipulation or blackmail, so most words are weapons, sometimes clumsy and obvious, sometimes complicated and tricky, but weapons nevertheless, designed to rob someone of their energy and their life force.

It became clear why language was poisonous. If the inadequacy of the words didn't hold one in ignorance long enough to decay and die, then the venomous energy behind the insults and threats delivered by negative people, designed to rob and steal, would soon finish a person off. So where lay the language of truth and creation?

I remembered Christ's words. He said that 'a man defiles himself from out of his mouth'. I took this to mean that if he is good then he can eat almost anything as food and transmute it. If he is bad, then the energy of his words will do untold damage to every life form around him, and eventually return to him tenfold, causing much pain and regret.

At this time I had my own late-night radio phone-in programme with a local radio station. People would ring in and ask a variety of questions about psychic subjects and I would try my best to answer them. The programme lasted from eleven in the evening until one in the morning and I never knew whether the questions would be straightforward or difficult. After one such programme, which had been surprisingly easy, apart from a couple of priests telling me that I was in league with Lucifer and all his little imps, I relaxed for a while with a cup of tea and a cigarette before leaving the studio to begin the fifteen-mile journey home towards Swindon.

I'd been driving for about ten minutes or so and was feeling fairly tired but happy. There was very little traffic at that time of the morning and the sky was clear with just a few wispy clouds drifting off to the west. I was feeling rather pleased with the way I had handled the broadcast and my mind scanned back over the various telephone conversations of the evening.

I had defeated several zealous religious callers by setting them the following riddle. 'In the beginning there was Adam and Eve. According to the Bible, they had two sons, Cain and Abel. Cain killed Abel and then, we are told, he went to the Land of Nod, east of Eden where he took for himself a wife. Who was she? After all, there were only three people left on the earth.'

It worked every time with people who quoted the Bible at me, as many did, but then I had the sense to realise that verbal fencing was no substitute for truth. People enjoyed word games. Language games, riddles and debates all belonged to the limitless mental plane where one could intellectualise anything forever, until of course one became old and died. I considered that with some people it would probably carry on even after that, and they would no doubt debate semantics with the very people who were trying to move them on and up through the Universe.

Suddenly, I noticed a dazzling light in the sky to my left and for a split second I ignored it. Then I looked again and this time I thought, 'Good God – what is that?' I pulled the car over on to the grass verge of the road and climbed out. There was a pleasantly cool night breeze and the stars were clear and beautiful. The moon rested low in the sky behind me but above and in front of me was the most beautiful sight I have ever seen.

It was a mass of light. I counted one hundred and thirty-five individual coloured lights. Green, red, blue and yellow, all converging into a core of dazzling white light, the shape of which was strangely similar to the 'Enterprise' of Star Trek fame, a disc shape with huge, horizontal, cylindrical objects at the back, which I took to be engines.

I told myself that I was seeing things, that I had been overworking, worrying too much and eating the wrong foods. My mind followed trains of pragmatic thought in an effort to rationalise what I was seeing, but it just stayed there, and I stood beside the car, transfixed with awe and wonder.

When my mind finally quietened down, I could feel an unbelievable sense of peace flowing through me and a sensation of sheer beauty emanating from this awesome craft. Just for a moment, I was aware of people on board, many people, more superior and advanced than me, yet at the same time I could feel such overwhelming kindness and compassion emanating from them, almost as if their energies were healing me. I felt charmed and bewitched and blissfully happy and if someone had said to me in that moment, 'Come with us but you'll never see Earth again', I would have gone without a moment's hesitation for I felt so utterly safe.

It was real. The enormity of that realisation burned into my brain, and if it was, then I knew that there really was something out there better than the banks and the supermarkets, something more meaningful than simply eating and sleeping, struggling and worrying. I started to dance a jig around the car, for it was one thing to guess or to wonder or to contemplate such things, that's just a mental exercise, a fantasy woven around wishful thinking and nothing really changes, but this beautiful starship had changed everything. This was real and I felt certain that I'd never be the same again.

I wasn't arrogant enough to think that it was there specifically 'for me' but I felt certain it was on some sort of mission. It was obviously pausing on a journey and the occupants were probably totally unaware of me, but I'd seen it and it had changed my life. After that, I stopped worrying so much about everything. Maybe that's what I was meant to learn from the observation. That worry has about as much value as beating oneself over the head with a stick. Much better to put the energy to good use by attacking the causes of worry and defeating them.

I drove back into Swindon in a dreamy haze. The craft had still been clearly visible when I'd decided to leave, but the cold had forced me to move eventually. When I'd tried to start the car, I found the battery was almost flat and there was only just enough power to start the engine. I noticed too that the car was charged with static electricity, which made my clothing crackle when it touched the metal. Never mind; I was high on a new sense of freedom and I eventually reached home and collapsed into bed, aware that there was an inane grin on my face as I fell into a deep sleep.

A few nights later, Lilith came back into my dreams.

'Congratulations,' she said. 'You're not as primitive as you look. Can't stay too long; I'm going to a party.'

'You mean you go to parties?'

She placed her hands on her hips and glared at me patronisingly.

'What do you think I do with my time? You're so ignorant that you aren't even aware of the existence of inter-stellar life. I do have a home, you know, and friends. I eat and drink and I have fun just the same as you do. Well, assuming that what you do in your life could remotely be classified as fun. It just so happens that I don't live in or on your world, that's all.

'I have to go and change now. Oh, by the way, did you realise that the reason my clothes always seem dark to you is because of your limited visual spectrum? I shall be wearing a turquoise dress to the party later on and I'm really looking forward to going, so listen carefully, little brain.'

'Why are you always so rude?' I asked her petulantly. 'Is it really necessary?'

'I'm self-taught,' she retorted, pulling a small mirror from a pocket and studying her white face.

'Language,' she went on, 'should aspire towards perfect communication, which is truly represented only by feelings. The mind responds instantly to the inherent meaning of words and tends to create its own reality, whereas feelings are universal and always totally honest. One cannot lie with a feeling. Therefore, whenever people are communicating with each other, they should try to push the feeling towards the person with whom they are communicating. That way they will merge with the person, learn what it feels like to be them and understand them better.

'Also, it is important to recognise one's own "true feelings" and thus have a correct dialogue with oneself, so that disease and depression do not have a chance to gain a foothold in one's mind or psyche. If the observed feeling is negative, one can begin to transmute the energy contained within it instantly and thereby remain unpolluted – do you follow?' I nodded. 'And does my make-up look all right?'

'Make-up!' I exclaimed in disbelief.

'Oh, not the same rubbish that women use here, that poison simply blocks the pores of the skin and prevents it from breathing, no, I use far more evolved creations, cellular energy-enhancing substances.'

'You look wonderful,' I said.

'Good, it's nice to be appreciated. It's a pity that you're so unevolved, otherwise you could have come with me. Unfortunately, you'd be bound to say something completely stupid because most of your comments come from prejudice, bigotry and fear. Apart from that, most of my friends telepathise in part, which you are unable to do, because you use only a tiny portion of your brain. You would panic as soon as you discovered that they could detect all the dark, seedy little thoughts lurking around in your brain concerning lust and greed and self-image.

'Also,' here she made a face at me, 'I'm sorry to say it, but you are very scruffy and badly dressed and the material of your clothes would be quite unsuitable.

'Neither would you like any of the food as your taste buds are programmed by laziness only to accept sweet or highly spiced comforting foods, whereas the food at the party, having a very high energy and nutritional content, would taste like horse-shit to you and you would gag and show me up. You might also feel a bit inferior, when you're surrounded by people who use at least forty per cent of their brains, when you struggle to use five. Then you'd get scared because you'd want to know exactly where you were as humans always do, and once you discovered that you weren't on good old comfortable Earth, you'd probably freak out, have a panic attack and run around in circles. Apart from the obvious problem of getting your basic cells up to a high enough frequency for you to travel there at all. Better that you stay in bed and rest your fear-filled brain.'

I couldn't help smiling at her insults, which carried no insulting energy at all.

'I could try,' I protested.

She stared at me long and hard, then she shrugged her shoulders, flicked her hair into shape with her fingers and said, 'OK, but you'd better behave yourself. No primitive behaviour, otherwise you're dead, and I mean dead as in really horrible, dark, spooky broom cupboard crying in the middle of the night dead.'

The dream changed and I was in a warm comfortable room with a red carpet and pink walls hung with the most weird and wonderful paintings. The furniture was plush and inviting, the lighting soft, and beautiful haunting music was playing quietly in the background. There were about twenty people in the room, some sitting and some standing, most holding tall, thin glasses, all chatting happily and laughing. They all looked incredibly healthy and relaxed.

A man walked up to me and shook me warmly by the hand; and his energy washed over me and I felt instantly at ease.

'Hi,' he said. 'I'm Mark. You must be on your way up, you know, working your way up through the Universe. Congratulations, good to have you here.' I stared at him like a half-wit with my mouth partly open. Lilith ground the heel of her shoe hard into my right foot until I winced with pain.

'Think something intelligent,' she whispered, and I thought, 'Well, I may be thick but I'm trying, and that's the best I can do.'

'Darn right it is,' exclaimed Mark. 'Everyone loves a trier.' He put his arm around my shoulder and led me towards the others. 'One day I'll tell you about my thick lifetimes; boy, was I stupid, you'll die laughing. Took me absolutely ages to catch on.'

He escorted me around the room and introduced me to everyone, and I didn't say a word, but every time I thought something, they answered. I quickly learnt to think things that were totally honest and my confidence grew and grew.

A woman called Marinette, wearing a long, beautiful, deep-blue gown, approached me with an unusual drink in a tall delicate glass.

'Your knowledge of botany is limited,' she said with a smile, 'but trust me. I know this is new to you but I think you'll like it.'

I did like it very much but the energy of the liquid set my head spinning.

'Don't be afraid of the effects on your body,' she said. 'Go with the energy of the drink instead of fighting against it and you'll feel fine.'

I did as she advised and my head cleared instantly.

'In your world,' she went on, 'you'd have to be aware of whether the drink was, in your terms, good or bad for your body cells, but here there isn't that problem; everything here is good for you.'

I thought, 'But then, what problems do you have to work through or on?'

'Internal ones,' she answered smiling. 'Inner fears mostly; the difference here is that no negative energy is projected outwards, so everything around us is free to grow, just as we ourselves are free to grow.'

'And you have plants and animals here, the same as on Earth, but different, of course?' I thought.

'Oh yes,' she smiled.

I found myself automatically thinking, 'I would like to go now. It's been a pleasure to meet you all and I'm sincerely grateful for being allowed to come here, but I feel that now I'm starting to need, and as I need, I take, and I wish only to give.'

Instantly the dream ended. I awoke late, with the sunlight streaming into my bedroom, a dishevelled human being wrestling with a twisted quilt. I managed to smile, because I'd understood language in its purest sense, the sense of automatic energy interaction. Now I knew that, in a perfect world, there was no need to say anything. Speech was just a contrivance to ease the discomfort of clumsy understanding. Total awareness of the nature of one's feelings was all that was required, for that embodied complete honesty, which harms nothing and no-one and which gives everyone a truth to which they can positively respond.

WE WOULD OFTEN BE SORRY

IF OUR WISHES

WERE GRATIFIED

Aesop

# Chapter Eight

## Descent into Goblin City

Lilith came into my dreams three nights later and seemed strangely cool and stand-offish.

'You did very well,' she said stiffly, but her eyes were sad and her body language awkward and agitated. 'You recognised the exact moment when you began to drain people's energies and then you graciously took your leave. I was proud of you for that; it showed great promise.'

'Why are you so sad?' I asked.

'I'm not sad,' she snapped back. 'Have you yet to realise how powerful and evolved I am? I don't get sad, only unevolved creatures like you get sad. Sad at your own faults and failings and your inability to deal with fear. Please don't speak such rubbish to me.'

Yet she was almost crying. I had never seen her upset before and my empathy towards her almost broke my heart.

'I must have done something wrong for you to be so distressed,' I said quietly.

'No,' she murmured, 'you did not do anything wrong.'

'Then what is wrong?'

'I am in a tail-spin,' she said hesitantly. 'I am losing myself, I am losing me. Everything is becoming so very base, dark and heavy, and I'm so frightened. Fear has always frightened me; I am not accustomed to it. It is so

long since I have felt it – centuries, in fact – and yet now it
gnaws at my stomach and tightens my throat. It makes
my mind spin and it holds me.'

'Can you explain more?' I asked, genuinely trying to
understand.

'As I become more negative,' she explained, 'my
cellular frequency drops, therefore my atomic weight
rises. Earth gravity then exerts a greater pull on my dense
matter body and prevents me from going home. Also, as
the cellular frequency drops, the quality of my thinking
drops and my thoughts become more and more basic,
unevolved and aggressive. Fear always manifests as
anger, therefore soon I will insult you more and more,
and unless I can manage to raise my energies or
transcend or transmute my mood, then I will certainly
attack you.'

'I understand,' I said, 'but what triggered this, er – tail-
spin?'

'It doesn't matter,' she said sadly.

'Of course it matters!' I exclaimed, trying to keep her in
a good humour, 'if it is having this devastating effect on
you.'

'It doesn't matter,' she repeated.

'Tell me,' I said. She began to cry. I was shocked to see
her apparently helpless and almost inferior to me.

'I am trapped,' she said quietly, 'in the inner circle of
my own negative thoughts. I cannot go home, my friends
cannot reach me. I am lost in a strange place. I have no
power – I cannot see and I cannot hear …'

'That doesn't answer my question,' I said.

'What question?' she asked tearfully.

'What triggered this tail-spin?'

She floundered around for a few moments, then held
her head in her hands and shook it from side to side.

'I was jealous,' she whispered.

I smiled kindly. 'Jealous of what?'

She bowed her head and turned quite pale. 'Of you and Marinette, at the party.'

'But I felt no fondness for Marinette,' I protested.

'Oh, I know, I know,' she said, with tears trickling down her cheeks, 'but she was fond of you, and your energies are more compatible with hers than with my own.'

'But she isn't you,' I said softly.

'That's precisely the problem,' she whispered, almost managing a faint smile.

'No, no, no, I mean, she isn't you.'

'You just said that, have you become a half-wit?'

'Perhaps, but I don't think so. I was a half-wit once, but you changed all that; you changed everything about me. You have made me whatever I am now, but whoever I have become, I am still an individual and I know my own soul and my own heart and I know whom I love.'

'So do I,' she said. 'Energy follows thought. Marinette's fondness for you will grow to affection and then to love, and it will pull you, call to you and enchant you, and then she'll want to take over teaching you on the grounds that there exists a mutual bond between you, and she'll get her own way, she always does!'

'But it's you that I love,' I said emphatically.

She blinked at me. 'And do you know enough about yourself to be able to say that truthfully?' she asked.

'Of course.'

'But I'm a hard bitch.'

'I know.'

'Then how do I possibly attract you – are you mad?'

'Look,' I said persistently, 'you are allowing your fears to overtake you. If you focus on your fears you will become lost in a thousand dark moments, and in that confused state you will completely forget that I have free will, to like and love whom I choose.'

She sniffed and glared at me. 'Well, listen to the Buddha boy,' she sneered. 'I must say that this is the first time that chocolate, cigarettes, Valium and booze have ever made anyone enlightened. Don't you dare preach to me. I was aware and evolved while you were still catching your dinner with a spear in the aftermath of the Matriarchal Age, in the middle of the Dark Ages, when you were a toothless wonder who worshipped lightning. I, on the other hand, am almost omnipotent.'

'You have no reason to be jealous,' I said calmly.

'Don't patronise me, you worm, you great big pile of dung.'

'Oh dear,' I said, 'gravity is getting a real hold on you. Your flesh will be as dense as mine soon. Please be careful, this is a heavy world, you know.'

'Well, thank you, Einstein! But the bottom line is that Marinette wasn't a million light-years off shagging you, 'cos she fancied a bit of unevolved rough. That's the sort of tart she is, the common old bag, unevolved cow, the stupid, ugly, arrogant, insidious bitch – and another thing …' She stopped suddenly and looked very frightened and stuck her thumb in her mouth like a child. There was a long silence.

'Karma,' she whispered finally, 'I've created karma for myself.'

'No, you haven't,' I comforted. 'There was no negative venom in your words, no pollution, therefore I'm sure Marinette will understand.'

'Do you really think so, honestly?'

'I'm sure of it,' I answered. There was another long silence, and then she looked at me pleadingly.

'I can't move,' she whispered.

'That's because you now weigh about eighteen stone,' I said 'You must change your mindset fast.'

'Shit, shit – shit – HELP!'

'You've devolved,' I said. 'You're glued to the earth by your own high atomic weight. You have the same volume, but your mass and weight have soared.'

'I know all that crap!' she protested. 'I teach it – remember? I am the boss here, not you. Now I order you to get me out of this mess immediately. I don't want to be stuck here on this awful planet, surrounded by all these horrible people, who smell and who don't know anything – do something!'

'Try a mantra,' I suggested.

'Up your bum,' she shouted.

'No,' I said, 'that's not a good mantra; that will only make things worse.'

'Don't like mantras,' she scowled. 'Never could handle sodding stupid mantras. Repeating Om mani padme hum over and over again like a stupid, demented parrot. Think of something else, quickly, I swear I'm getting even heavier!'

'Deep breathing!' I exclaimed with a rush of inspiration.

'Oh, shit off!' she groaned. 'What, deep breathing, with this air! Air that is full of shit, chemical shit, decaying proteins from dead skin cells and the vile low energy breath of people. Me, breathe that, you have to be joking! I am a high priestess. I am a queen. I am an incredibly evolved life form. I'd have to work like some demented yogic master to transmute the crappy air that I have to breathe when I'm here, without your suggesting that I take in huge lungfuls of the stuff. Just bloody well think of something – slave!'

'So you had slaves around in the time when I was catching my dinner with a spear,' I smiled.

'Of course! Well, they weren't fit for anything else. It was an honour for them to serve me; gave a purpose to their sad, meaningless lives.'

'Oh dear,' I said. 'You are devolving fast. You must be almost twenty stone by now. You'll start increasing in volume soon, because the energy will become gas, and then liquid, and finally solid fat, especially since you regenerate your cells so fast, you being such a highly evolved being and all.'

'Me – be FAT!' she almost screamed in horror. 'Me – FAT, I can't be FAT. I must never be fat, I am beautiful, so very beautiful! I've always been beautiful! Oh please, anything but fat. I've always had a body that sank a thousand ships, no, that's wrong, my face sank a thousand ships, no, wrong again – oh dear, oh dear.'

I managed with a struggle somehow to lift her on to a dream sofa, and sat down beside her. I put my arms around her, even though she protested vigorously at being touched, spat at me and called me names.

'Now project all the negative energy into me,' I said.

'Can't do that,' she said, 'you'll become ill, very ill.'

'I don't care,' I insisted. 'Just do it.'

She protested further with a string of 'buts', so I just kept repeating, 'just do it please' until her resolve weakened and my own free will held sway over her. Then suddenly she couldn't hold the negative energy any longer, and it moved into me accompanied by one huge burp from her, which embarrassed her greatly.

'By the way,' she said stiffly, 'I didn't plan on your learning it this way, it is most inefficient of me, but the sixth deadly venom is GRAVITY.'

After this dream I was ill for a month with a serious throat infection. Doctors came and went, as did various alternative practitioners whom I knew, and the antibiotics became stronger and stronger. I was feverish for most of the time and often hallucinated. During one such episode a young woman appeared beside the bed, with short black hair and wearing a smart black suit, which bore small silver insignia like those of an army uniform, and she was studying a sort of electronic clipboard. Her manner was very stiff and proper.

She said, 'You are ...' and then proceeded to recite a very long number at incredible speed, until my hot and sore brain began to hurt.

'This is your DNA "bar code", so to speak,' she went on. 'It identifies you as a Universal, individual life form, and you have been toxically polluted by ...' and then she proceeded to relate to me another stream of numbers, different of course from my own, until the pain in my head became almost unbearable.

'You mean Lilith?' I said.

'That does not compute,' she said. 'I use sixty-seven per cent of my brain, and I only read, recognise and understand numbers. Now I am a very busy individual and it is enormously difficult for me to survive in this hostile environment for any length of time, especially close to you with your extremely negative energies affecting my person.

'Also, it is very painful to communicate my energy to you in such a way that you can perceive it in your language. So, I need to know, do you wish the energy that is contaminating you to be returned to source?'

'No,' I said briefly.

'You do understand the question?'

'Yes. Thank you. With my pathetic five-per-cent brain, I do understand.'

'Very well.' She paused to make entries into her computerised clipboard. 'It is so noted. Your percentage chance of physical survival, that is, the recovery and continuity of your present body, is seventy-two point three zero zero zero one.'

'Thank you,' I said, 'that is very comforting.' She simply blinked at me.

'Are you real?' I asked. 'Or are you an hallucination caused by fever?'

'I am "real",' she sighed, 'as you put it, to any life form that shares my cellular frequency. Since you obviously do not, then no, using your primitive language, I am not real. Goodbye.'

I took some more antibiotics. I wished I could have seen the doctor who used to visit me whenever I had been ill as a child, an old Scottish gentleman called Dr Moffat. He would always give me a bottle of pink liquid, which tasted like chalk and which seemed to cure everything, and a bottle of red, cherry-flavoured liquid that he called a tonic. I had always felt that he could cure anything so I had been shocked and saddened when he died. I remembered him as a wise and kindly man who had never been in a hurry and who had always made me feel that he cared deeply for me.

Although I was very slow to recover, secretly I was quite pleased and flattered to have been polluted by Lilith's energies. She was, after all, a very important personage who had appeared in historical and mythological archives time and time again in one guise or another. Even though the feeling seemed slightly perverse, it was also very loving and created a powerful sensation of loyalty towards her.

I often drove to the countryside to get as much fresh air as possible. As I rested and recuperated I had plenty of time in which to ponder all that had happened to me and all that I had learnt.

I realised that the density and frequency of the sub-atomic particles that comprised my cells could be altered, either by other people's energies or by my own negativity, and that the density and frequency would rise and fall accordingly.

If the frequencies rose, then my cells would regenerate faster; my atomic weight would drop and gravity could not then affect me so much, thus easing the pull on my muscles and the dragging-down effect upon my bodily organs. I would then be able to move faster, think faster, sleep less and just generally feel amazing.

If my frequencies fell, however, through my own fear or external negative influences, then the atomic weight would rise, gravity would hold me tightly, I would feel slow and tired and my thinking would become very moronic.

I realised, for example, that if everyone aboard the Titanic could have somehow entered a state of yogic meditation just after the ship had hit the iceberg, then the sum total of their bodily weight would not have risen and their energies would not have increased the atomic weight of the structure and fabric of the ship. This would have meant that, although it would still have gone down because metal is denser than water, nevertheless the ship might have stayed afloat long enough for a rescue ship to arrive.

I also played around with Newtonian physics, and while accepting that an apple falls to Earth (after, we are told, bouncing off Newton's head!) at a fixed rate of acceleration due to gravity of thirty-two feet per second squared, I decided that this formula was true only if certain finer constants were in operation. The atomic frequency and weight of the apple, the density of the air and the frequency of the energy emanating from Newton himself could all be altered and therefore affect the result of the experiment. If negative people had surrounded Newton at the time, then their energies would have made the air and the apple 'heavy' and it would have been pulled towards the Earth much faster. Conversely, had very advanced people surrounded him, then the reverse would have been true and the apple would have moved much more slowly towards the ground.

Then the metaphorical penny dropped in my brain, not at any fixed rate of acceleration either – I realised that it was possible to fly!

As a child I had often made a complete fool of myself by running along the streets, flapping my arms vigorously in the vain hope that I would take off and then soar like an eagle. For obvious reasons I never did, but I figured that if somehow I could have raised my frequencies to such a degree that gravity exerted a minimal pull on my body, then I would be able to move through the air quite easily – provided that I felt no fear, which would have made me drop like a stone.

I called this my 'floating apple theory'.

I was quickly overwhelmed by the realisation of the amount of work and effort it would take to raise my frequencies to such a high level, and I understood why martial arts experts spent years, maybe their whole early lives, training in Tibetan temples. Going through one's fear in order to raise perception seemed a fine concept, but in practice it would be an awesome task just to go through and conquer even a relatively small fear and to enjoy the ensuing benefits. I pondered how many years of yogic breathing it would take just to lighten myself even slightly. I smiled. The task was monumental, but at least I understood the theory.

Although science can often present itself as an almost god-like mystery, conducted by very clever people who do great good most of the time, the fact remains that negative people literally 'bring you down'. So, is this simply sociology? If so, then logically one has to conclude that health, happiness and eternal youth are simply pleasant concepts, but if it is science, then logic dictates that such things are our natural state of being, long lost, and all to be regained.

Christ walked on water because His cellular frequency was the same or higher than water. Saint Peter sank because his fear lowered his cellular frequency and increased his atomic weight. Ultimately both science and sociology are outdated concepts. The energetics of the experiment and the experimenter become one. All things interact and, as we learn to inter-react in an ever more conscious way, the true nature of our being becomes evident.

IT IS THE COMMONEST OF

MISTAKES TO CONSIDER THAT

THE LIMIT OF OUR POWER

OF PERCEPTION IS ALSO

THE LIMIT OF ALL THERE

IS TO PERCEIVE

C. W. Leadbeater

# Chapter Nine

## Back to the future

I hadn't dreamt of Lilith for months and I began to miss her intensely. It seemed insane to be in love with someone who existed in dream states, but I realised that I was in love with her. I tried projecting loving energy towards her and messages in the form of imaginary distress flares, but no answers came.

Sometimes I would drive to my beloved Avebury at night simply to gaze at the stars and smell the subtle scents of foliage on the gentle night breezes. I loved to walk around and around the stone circles, touching the stones, feeling the magical energy of them, some male, some female, but all of them powerful and friendly, yet all the time I wondered where Lilith might be, and still no dreams came.

I felt so very alone, and everyone seemed so dull compared to her. People on the streets, people in shops, people everywhere, seemed so slow and heavy and negative. Everything they did seemed to happen in slow motion as they clawed painfully through their fears, the dense nature of their bodies and the chaos of their minds, to struggle haplessly towards yet another predictable day. They seemed to me like half-people, halflings or half-finished sculptures that inhabited an almost alien world of shadows and dubious realities.

I tried to buy and sell antiques but the greed and avarice of it all offended me. I worked in various offices but became bored by the pointless movement of paper and by the inevitable office politics. My unpleasant experiences in the solicitor's office had been quite enough for one lifetime, although it had taught me endurance, but now my life was drifting and without purpose, and the strain on my mood and demeanour was starting to show.

I began reading tarot cards for people and sometimes healing them 'hands on' by removing negative energies from their bodies and replacing them with good positive energies. This was very successful and I met some delightful people. Then, suddenly, when I had almost resigned myself to being abandoned by the Universe, the dreams came once again.

I dreamt I was a soldier dressed in an old-fashioned blue uniform. I'd been summoned from the hot, dusty barrack-room to stand to attention before a commanding officer who was hard-faced and stocky, with jet-black hair and a large moustache. He was impeccably smart, and his clear blue eyes missed nothing.

'You live in a heavy world,' he said finally, leaning back in his large, comfortable chair. 'Communication is hard for you, I realise that, and a sense of purpose even harder.' He paused. 'The people of your world are so very isolated,' he said in what seemed like a sad voice. 'This is why we prefer to communicate through dreams. It involves less risk of pollution for us. Nevertheless, we are just like you. We look much the same, feel much the same. We have our homes and our friends and our loved ones, we just don't live on your planet. How old are you?'

'Thirty-five,' I answered.

'Thirty-five what!' he barked back at me.

'Thirty-five years,' I answered quickly and rather nervously.

'No,' he said, reproachfully and slowly. '"Thirty-five, sir". I am the officer on parade and you, even though you are a shabby disgrace to humanity, untidy, lazy, slow of mind and body, a very slovenly soldier indeed, are nevertheless a major in the Universal Police, therefore I would appreciate it if you would act like one. So straighten yourself up and at least try to look alive in my presence.' I obeyed immediately.

'That is slightly better,' he said, gazing at me disapprovingly. 'Now, let us begin again. How old are you?'

'Thirty-five – sir!'

'No, try again.'

'Thirty-five years – sir!'

'Define a year?'

'Twelve months or fifty-two weeks or three hundred and sixty-five days – sir!' He leaned back in his chair, sighed deeply and shook his head.

'You talk absolute nonsense,' he said finally. 'I cannot understand you. Are you really so stupid?'

My mind began spinning and searching frantically for more correct answers, but he continued, 'I am not interested in your feeble intellectual concepts drawn on or from the perceptions and mental machinations of individuals from your history who perceived only small fragments of the truth.

'I want you to define a year in intelligent and accurate terms, in a way that I can understand. In other words, I want you to grow up, abandon your immature ideas and talk sense to me. Now try again. Define a year.'

There was a long silence while he impatiently tapped his pencil harder and harder on his desk.

'Four seasons,' I blurted out finally. 'Spring, summer, autumn and winter,' adding quickly, 'sir!'

'That answer does not make me as annoyed as your previous answers,' he said, 'but it still frustrates me greatly. I thought you had been trained up, but it certainly doesn't seem as though you have been. Can you not push your tired, lazy mind just one step further and give me an accurate answer?'

There was a long silence. I gradually came to realise that this dream was an interview, an examination of sorts, and that I was failing dismally, letting myself down and, worst of all, letting Lilith down. Even in a dream state I could feel my blood pressure rising and perspiration trickling down my forehead. I could also feel myself blushing. I knew I had to succeed. I had to get it right for Lilith and for myself, so I strained my brain until it hurt.

Finally I said, 'A year is an utterance, sir, the sound of which has meaning for people of my world. To those of little evolution it denotes the answers that I have already given, but to those who think and perceive life in a more evolved way, it denotes the movement of this planet, which is called Earth by its inhabitants, once around the nearest sun-star – sir!' The man almost smiled and leaned back in his chair again.

'An intelligent answer,' he observed, 'but still completely wrong. Do try again, bearing in mind that I do not have all the time in your world, or my own for that matter.'

I knew that I was on the right track. I just needed one more quantum leap of inspired logic, one more mental push.

'I asked how old you are,' he added, 'just to remind you of the original question.'

I suddenly realised that he meant 'including previous lifetimes', but how could I possibly remember those, let alone estimate the time span of each one and the time spaces in between each incarnation? My brain began to develop the worst dream-migraine of all time, and then I remembered that, although my mind may not remember, my spirit would, if I could just get out of my own way mentally and stop my mind chattering incessant fearful thoughts.

'I am one hundred and sixty-two thousand, three hundred and sixty-eight years old,' I said at last, without any idea of where the words had come from, 'a year being defined by my previous statement – sir!'

'Well, go on,' he said, 'I can see that you've had an inspired idea.'

'I've just realised, sir, that just as my DNA number identifies who I am, the number that I have just cited denotes when I am.'

'Good!' he exclaimed. 'At last. You see, your brain does work after all! Just to add, though, as I'm something of a perfectionist, that since your planet is constantly moving, your so-called age-number is also constantly changing. So you should allow for that shift in your answer and state it; but never mind, all that remains now is where you are, although since you use only five per cent of your brain I doubt if you'll be able to work that out.'

'I am at the magnetic and geometric centre created by the energies of life forms that surround me, sir. In other words, where I am is dictated by the flux in energies of my surroundings.'

'And could you prove that mathematically?'

'No, sir, I do not possess the necessary information or perception.'

'Nevertheless,' he said, with a faint smile of approval, 'it was a very good try, very inspired, and almost accurate. If we say that "everything is in its correct place", we must therefore consider the meaning and context of the word "correct". I am pleased. You have been trained well. I am more interested in your concepts of time than those of space, but to help you clarify your definition of where you are, I can tell you. You are in the Universal matrix. We are all co-existing in the Universal matrix.'

It was a strange contradiction the next morning to be eating my breakfast cereal on the one hand and considering the form and nature of the 'Universal matrix' on the other. I had become accustomed to dreams now, and I accepted them as meeting places between the evolved and the unevolved, I myself being in the latter group, of course.

I knew that the people in the dreams were real, with their own homes and friends and loved ones, somewhere 'out there', on far distant worlds, all kindly trying to improve this world by instructing a few of its inhabitants. So I felt very honoured but I never thought for one moment that I was the only person receiving such instructive dreams.

I realised also that the words 'evolved' and 'unevolved' were purely relative. I was evolved when compared to a thief or a violent thug, yet totally unevolved when compared to the people I was dreaming about, who were obviously far wiser and more perceptive than myself.

It will have become obvious by now that I have not included in this narrative the more mundane aspects of my life, choosing rather to concentrate on metaphysical subjects to give the reader the best chance of survival.

Life is, in a sense, a race against deadly venoms. We are born, we grow up. We must manage to get to grips and conquer the majority of in-bred poisons before we reach our optimum appearance, which is around twenty-nine years of age. If we fail to achieve this, then we are in grave danger of never getting ahead of our own destructive forces.

It is not easy to exist in society. Environmental pollution, the demands of relatives, the constant fight to earn a living and pay bills, the emotional needs of people close to us, the worry of social problems and national issues all combine to work against us. Survival is a lonely pursuit, since most people seem to have a morbid fascination with age and death and subscribe to both concepts by taking out pension schemes and funeral plans. It all drags us down and makes us feel isolated and somewhat helpless in our endeavours.

One could liken the mass of people to a herd of dinosaurs plodding across a prairie. The herd simply eats and drinks and sleeps. Some members of the herd fall into swamps and die, some are eaten, some die of old age, but these are replaced by younger dinosaurs, and so the herd marches on, without ever stopping to wonder if there is anything more to life. They say in effect, 'This is all there is, plodding, eating, drinking. We have never stopped to think. We have never questioned what we do because there is nothing beyond what we do; this is our existence.'

Should a dinosaur break away and discover a new and better way of life, it is not allowed to return and therefore cannot be listened to, so no progress is ever made and no conscious evolution ever takes place.

All the time that my understanding of the metaphysical world was growing through dreams, I was earning a living and paying my bills. I had a few casual friends and a few casual girlfriends, but all those aspects of my life are not important, since without survival everything else is completely academic.

It is interesting also how people react to numbers on a deep psychological level. When they reach twenty years of age, they fly into a panic to be successful or to get married. They dread being thirty, so they are never still or at peace within themselves. When they are thirty, the idea of being forty fills them with stark terror and if they're not both married and materially successful by then, their rush to achieve those objectives becomes desperate.

At forty, they consider life to be ebbing away and almost over, because they perceive fifty as the end. When fifty comes they settle down into a conditioned way of being towards sixty and beyond, hoping deep down for a painless and easy death. If they are married they secretly hope that they will die before their partner to avoid the pain of being 'left behind' and, in any event, they try to bluff everyone that they're not petrified.

There are people walking this world, beautiful, fresh, vital people, who are well over four thousand years old, or even much more, but you won't know, you won't recognise them, because you'll think that they are around twenty-nine. They won't approach you in the local pub or supermarket and tell you the truth about themselves because they will avoid negative, base energies as much as possible.

Why should they tell you anyway? They know what they know. They have discovered the secret of eternal youth, eternal health and they derive no benefit from telling you. Anyway, you wouldn't believe them if they did.

Just because the vast majority of people are locked rigidly into the linear time concept and the absolute belief in death doesn't mean that they are right. No more than the people who believed the Earth to be flat were right. However, even though they are wrong, the energy emanations of their beliefs are awesomely powerful and one has to challenge them, moment to moment, day by day, otherwise one will be drawn along with their beliefs until one is thinking 'survival' in a very half-hearted way while still paying lip-service to the entrenched beliefs of other people.

It takes more than psychological tricks and affirmations to counter this. It is not a game. Death is not a game. Wrinkles on the face and failed bodies are not a game. They are the sad conclusion to over-exposure from other people's wrong thinking and bad energy. They induce weariness and negative moods in us, and as soon as negative people see those effects in us they accuse us of being like them, and if we are like them – which to some extent we allow ourselves to be – we conclude that we might as well share their gloomy fate.

Age is not beautiful; it is a mockery of all that a person once was. It is a disease, the result of poisoning. It is fashionable now to see age as beautiful, but how can this be so when it is less than a person once was? If once a person could run like the wind and now can only hobble around with the aid of walking sticks, how can that be beautiful or better?

People accept it because they have no choice. They have left it too late to think of a way out so they have to see it as a natural progression, an inevitability. They dress it up with quaint philosophies and so-called homely wisdom but, given the chance, they would choose to run again, and love again, and feel again – and they can!

But they must fight, fight the effects of the venoms. They must not drift into the thinking patterns of other people as a person dying of cold is tempted to fall into a sleep from which he will never wake, at least not in the same body.

Death is not beautiful. It is murder or, at best, manslaughter. It is a crime that unaware people commit upon each other and upon animals and plants, by failing to take responsibility for their own negative energies.

Death is terrifying, dark, forbidding and it rips the heart out of people who grieve. It has no dignity and no pride. It is a mark of failure, human life support systems failing owing to excessive pollution.

Why should death be inevitable when every cell in the body reproduces itself? What is the point of cells reproducing if death is a natural part of life? People write about it and try to 'tone it down'. They formulate clever sayings and phrases to make people believe that it isn't so bad. It's OK, they say, once you've accepted it and come to terms with the inevitability of it, you won't be terrified. In fact, then, you'll quite enjoy it. It has a serene sort of beauty; it is a doorway from one room to another.

Yet again, people accept this because they have no choice, and a whole folklore of ideas has been built up to make this ugly single option a slightly easier pill to swallow, but have any of the people who created these ideas survived to tell the tale? And all the helpers, counsellors and doctors who talk about the process as it unfolds around its victim – will they survive also? No, it is all guesswork on the part of people who do not know what to say. But it need not be so. It is your choice, and the humble purpose of this book is, for the first time, to give you a choice.

Anyone who believes that visible age and death are inevitable is wrong. Do not believe them. Fight the mass consciousness, think, take a deep, deep breath, summon up all your courage and challenge the 'truth' that is told to you. It may be the truth for most people, but that does not make it right.

The plain truth is that even good-hearted, aware people eventually give up the ghost and the will to live, because the people around them have treated them so badly, but they can't say so. It is socially unacceptable and politically incorrect to say so. People treat one another dreadfully so our memories, which constitute our true perception of time, become littered with sadness and hurt.

We grow weary and disillusioned when once we laughed and danced and played with a light heart and a sparkle in our eyes, when we were once so innocent. So what has happened? What has happened is all that people have done to us or, sometimes, what we have done to ourselves. That is what has made the difference. That is why we don't dance any more or think about sex any more or laugh any more.

We all huddle together into a particular age category and 'do things' together to kill time and stop ourselves thinking about the future. We go on holidays together and we all try to persuade one another that we're not hurt and utterly saddened by the way we've been treated.

We must be honest with people and realise that self-deception is a luxury that we cannot afford. If the energies of a particular person make your stomach turn over, your breathing shallow and your mouth dry, then you are being polluted, so complain and tell him or avoid him, but don't say it's all right because it isn't all right. It is one more bit of poison that will contribute to your decline – the decline of your body and of the way you think and of the way you feel, forming a vicious and deadly circle.

If you are not respected, don't accept it. Don't dress it up in silly social excuses such as, 'Oh well, I probably asked for that', or 'So-and-so didn't know what she was doing'. Of course she knew, it's just that she didn't care. So tell her, discipline her, or move away, but do not accept it. Sometimes you will become unpopular, even ostracised, but you will stay alive and you will stay young and you will keep all your options.

Time for you will not be marked in years, it will be marked in events. In that year this happened and in this year that happened and, by the way, that date is my birthday. If most or half of those events are unpleasant you must get rid of them, otherwise they will convey to you the subtle message, 'If this is all there is, then what is the point of going on?' and you will allow yourself to be carried along by the concepts of other people because deep down you want 'out'.

You want 'out' because you don't want any more pain or hurt or sadness. You don't want to hear any more cruel or spiteful words. You don't want to be let down any more. People cause pain and hurt and sadness in you, either directly or through the consequences of their actions, the dreadful 'ripple effects' of wicked intentions.

For example, a young man who breaks into your home and steals your video recorder may or may not be wicked. He may be a drug addict desperate for a 'fix'. The drug-pusher may have hooked him on drugs in the first place, in which case it is the drug-pusher who is responsible for the invasion of your property and the theft of your video recorder and the karma is attributable to him.

The Universe does not want you to die. Your body was not built to die. The people who run the Universe do not want you to die. Certainly YOU don't want to die, so get rid of all the bad memories by any means available: all these memories are telling you is that people 'know not what they do'.

Time is simply the motion of the Earth around the sun and the motion of the Earth as it turns on its axis. Motion will not kill you, therefore time cannot kill you. Only people can kill you, so it is crucial to your survival how you evaluate the beliefs and energy emanations of others.

As I write this, I have some pollution, some damage to my cells, but I know how it occurred, why it happened and the precise nature of the negative energies I was exposed to in order to create these minor problems. Most of all I know who was the source of those energies. So gradually, instead of giving in to them and regarding them as 'progressive degeneration', I am transmuting them and eventually I will eradicate them, in spite of all the social pressures upon me and around me.

As you read this, you will be in the same situation, and you must therefore answer the questions I have answered. Do not fall into the trap of thinking that you are so many years old and everyone has something wrong with them at that age. Instead, work out who did it to you. Be totally honest, even if the answer is that you did it to yourself because of hurt or anger. Be totally honest. Self-honesty is the key to truth. When you know the origins and the reasons, then start to transmute them, leave them behind and get those energies out of yourself in any way that you can. Make your prime directive SURVIVAL.

Answer this one question: 'If you were immortal, what would you do with your time?' Truth is, if you're honest, you don't want to be immortal. It's a nice, quaint idea but you don't really want it – and why not? Because life embodies hurt and it embodies hurt because you don't stick up for yourself and you don't stick up for yourself because you fear being ostracised and hurt even more.

The memory of your life thus far is marked with hurtful events and negative people. The people who are telling you that hurt is all there is and that it happens to everyone are the very same people who will have caused the hurt. They will also say that the best one can hope for is to be lucky and to suffer a minimum of hurt, but nevertheless hurt will happen. You must get rid of the hurt and reclaim your power. Challenge the hurt and resist the people who cause it, who revel in it – and the prospect of being immortal will seem simply glorious!

I have a passion for life. I love to feel existence around me. I love to touch and interact with life in all its beautiful forms and aspects. I love to smile and to laugh. I love to see and hear and breathe. I don't care what people have done to me. I will learn from it. I will sit in the eye of the hurricane at peace with myself.

I do not care what I have done to myself as I reacted to circumstances around me caused by other people. If I did bad things then I am sorry. I forgive myself. I forgive everyone. I don't care about hurt any more; it has no place in my memory and no part in me. I let it all go with awareness, blessed as valuable lessons. I don't care about pain any more, and all because life is simply too exciting and too beautiful to be bothered by such things.

I dreamt once more of the army officer. It was the same scenario as before. He was leaning back in his chair and studying me closely.

'I am here,' he said, tapping his pencil on the desk, 'to instruct you in the seventh deadly venom, which is TIME. Now, how old do you think I am?

'I do not have the necessary information regarding the motion of your home planet in order to give you a correct answer, sir!'

'Wrong,' he said quietly. 'Try again.'

I felt the beginnings of another dream-migraine and I began to perspire. The precise wording of his question ran through my mind over and over again, until I blurted out –

'I think you are very old, sir,' just managing to realise that the fulcrum of the question was the word 'think'.

'Good,' he said, smiling. 'That is much better. You actually heard what you listened to. Now, all you have to do is to see what you look at. Lilith taught you to do that, did she not? Well then, now do it. Look at me and tell me how old you think I am.'

'I have changed my mind, sir. I do not think you are very old at all.'

'And why is that?'

'Because you do not look old, sir!'

'Why?'

'Because your skin looks young and, with respect, sir, fresh.'

'Why?'

'Because, sir, the cells of your skin and also those of your internal organs are reproducing very fast.'

'Why? Keep going.'

I hesitated, one logical step away, one small leap of faith and reason and inspiration.

'Because you are not polluted by negative energy, sir!'

'Good,' he said. 'Very good indeed. Lilith trained you well; but there remains just one last question. How old do you think I am now, in the light of reason?'

I agonised, perspiring heavily, and then I smiled, a long deep smile. I felt like shouting out 'eureka!'. It was such an amazingly beautiful truth, such an ecstatic conclusion.

'I think, sir,' I said with an note of triumph in my voice, 'that the words "old" and "young" have no meaning for you whatsoever. You have transcended them. You are as you are perpetually because you have no pollution to hinder the correct reproduction of your cells. Therefore your body can self-regenerate as it was designed to do. You simply are as you wish to be, and nothing and no-one can destroy you. Tomorrow may have events for you to experience that are different from those you have experienced today, but you will be exactly the same because you take responsibility for all your events.'

'I create my own events,' he corrected.

'Yes, sir, I understand.'

'I believe that you do,' he smiled. 'I believe that you do. Now sleep, dream your own dreams and awake happy and refreshed.'

From then on I became a person who recorded events. There were no minutes or hours, no weeks, months or years, no yesterday, today or tomorrow, there were only events. If the events pleased me then I blessed them and understood them and put them into the treasure store of my soul. If the events did not please me, then I studied why they had been unpleasant, discovered whose energies had created them and learnt from them. When I was sure that I'd learnt each lesson then I consciously forgot the event, leaving my mind free for new pleasures and my body free of restrictive and harmful energies.

I ceased to think in terms of night and day and of seasons. I simply observed the passage of the Earth and thought how beautiful such motion and each position was. I did not always sleep through the night as other people had to do. At night the Earth was still moving; the geographical part of it, which I occupied, had simply turned away from the sun, creating another event.

Night was a cool and refreshing event and day was a warm, dynamic event full of bustle and promise. I realised that motion was always marked by events and that events could not occur without motion. I had evolved away from the notion of time.

However, in the day following that particular dream, when I tried to function in the so-called 'real world', it was almost impossible to maintain my new-found elation in the face of so many people who believed in an entirely different concept, the old way of thinking, the illogical idea of existing within a linear time frame.

They all believed, without question, that they were moving from somewhere towards somewhere else, and that ahead of them lay only loss, decay, illness and death. I found it all so offensive and primitive that I quickly became tired, and when all my work was finished and I'd eaten a simple meal, I collapsed exhausted into bed.

Lilith came in the night. She appeared very regal, dressed in a long flowing cloak the colour of port wine and boots that seemed almost 17th-century in style, of the type a highwayman might have worn.

'You did very well,' she said softly, 'and you did not let me down. Your examiner was very pleased.'

'You look different somehow,' I observed.

'No,' she smiled. 'I have always been the same, it is you who are changing. Now you see me more as I really am. You are not so frightened. You are wiser so I can be, as you might say, more myself.'

She paused and breathed deeply and appeared to be sitting on the side of my bed with her legs crossed, even though the whole scenario was a dream. I wondered if, as my fear levels dropped and my energy frequencies rose, the gap between us might start to close so that she could then draw closer to me, for now she seemed so real that I felt I could have reached out and touched her.

'Now you must listen very carefully,' she went on. 'Do not say anything, just listen. Things have become serious now and your mind has been well instructed in enlightened ideas, but you must realise that they are not simply ideas. You must make them a working reality, otherwise you will surely die of intellectualism.'

She paused again and seemed to glance at the curtained window. There was a faint blue light around her body, which enhanced her beauty.

'And yes,' she said, 'since you mentioned it in your mind, you could reach out and touch me right now, but you must not do so, it is not the right time.' She took a long, slow, deep breath. 'There is a secret you must know,' she said profoundly. 'Ignorance of it will kill you, so pay attention.'

She paused and then spoke more slowly, obviously choosing her words with great care.

'When the Matriarchal Age was about to fall, the army, which I commanded, divided into two parts. One half escorted the priestesses and as many priceless artifacts as possible eastwards and then north to seek safety in the high mountains, while the remaining part prepared to face the oncoming barbarians.

'These barbarians, or Chango people, took no prisoners. They did not even stop to save their wounded. They were primitive, unevolved killers and when they had sacked Delphi, they swept south and then veered east towards us, and we made our stand against them beside the eastern shores of the Red Sea.

'The battle lasted for three days and three nights. We could not hope to win because we were so greatly outnumbered. They fielded two million cavalry with countless foot soldiers following on behind, a sea of warriors like locusts over the land. Rather, we knew we could only delay them long enough for the first army to get far, far away.

'I died there, beside the shores of the Red Sea, and the Great Sphinx marks the place where I fell in battle and is also the tomb of the body which I lost then. I have not died since and I will not do so again.

'You were riding with the first army on escort duty. I ordered you to be there because you are a very good bodyguard. It broke your heart not to be with me, but you obeyed orders and you did your duty and you did it well.

'When the Chango people had conquered, all the various dark warlords divided the land up between themselves and so we saw the beginnings of violent and gruesome city-states all competing for power and domination. We also saw the beginnings of the patriarchal priesthoods who gave terrible names to huge grotesque figures of stone and forced ordinary people to worship them.

'They feared only one thing, the return of feminine power, the rise of Nemesis. So women were oppressed and treated like cattle until they gradually forgot all that they had once been. Events came and went; remember, history is simply a succession of events, and the events of the future depend on the things we do now; we create our own future.

'A species, through its group consciousness, creates its own reality. You must never again use the word "time". That word is forbidden to you. It is inappropriate. You speak and think events from now on. However, the early city–states with their accompanying priesthoods gradually began to feel more secure in their power, and the various religions became more sophisticated and subtle.

'Man had to control women, to ensure that they never remembered the glories of their past. Also, brutal man had to control the kindly man and the learned man and the wise man.

'Anyone who posed a threat to the evil and ruthless patriarchal regimes was brutally tortured and killed and used as a public example to warn off any would-be dissidents. But gradually this way of behaving became too obvious, the people had to be fooled into thinking that their overlords were right and good so a new system of control had to be found.

'Just because the rulers were evil does not mean they were stupid. On the contrary, they pondered long and hard upon the mysteries of existence to make themselves even more powerful and indestructible and, working with the priests, they discovered the inherent coding in the very essence of people, which you today call DNA.

'They symbolised it with the image of the serpent. Thus, the story woven around the Garden of Eden refers to a female rebellion and an attempt to reclaim the secret of feminine redemption, for which of course women are punished even more by the new male "god", and the rulers realised that this essence, the essential coding of people, was fluid and could be altered.'

She stretched and stroked her hands over her legs as I continued to listen, totally entranced by her words.

'So, they wrote into a so-called holy book that man has but three score years and ten upon this Earth and then he dies and returns to dust. People were uneducated and mostly illiterate, and anyone who wasn't – and who wasn't also corrupt and evil – was killed, so gradually people began to believe the lie.

'They were told that God wrote this book and that they had to believe it. Anyone who did not believe it was killed and so, through terror, this dreadful lie entered the coded essence of both man and woman and everyone began to die around that age because their cells now contained a little coded self-destruct instruction.

'As generations came and went, this signal became even more fixed and rooted in the cells of people. Children were obviously born with it, and they passed it on to their children and so on – and this is what Christ referred to as "original sin". Also His reference to "the sins of the fathers being visited on the children" refers partly to this and partly to the laws of karma. Remember that the word "sin", correctly translated, means "that which is not well for you" – quite different from the accepted meaning.

'You must understand, absolutely and truly, that all people have been controlled in this way since the collapse of the Matriarchal Age. To the unenlightened person, seventy orbits of the Earth around its sun-star is long enough to produce children who in turn become slaves, and long enough to work to promote the needs of the evil rulers; but it is not long enough for someone, using a tiny amount of perception, as they did in your history, to perceive the truth behind why events occurred and why they could never escape from the miserable cycle of birth, a short hard life and then death.

'Whenever people began to really think and to reason in your history, the rulers have always started a conflict or war to distract them. Ordinary people have always been distracted because people who think deeply are very dangerous to their masters. This is why education was so long in coming to you all, and why women especially were denied education.

'If you can't be killed in a war or be wounded and have your life ruined from then on, and if you can't be distracted, then the modern tactic is to amuse you so that you lose yourself in leisure. You are allowed to believe that you are wealthy enough to have a degree of control over your own existence, but be very careful. All these illusions are fundamentally created to prevent people from realising that within their very cells lurks the seed of their own destruction.'

She threw back her head, tossing her hair; her eyes flashed and she pointed an elegant finger at me.

'Reclaim your power,' she said loudly and coldly. 'God did not write the holy books. Brutal men wrote them, and they wrote them to serve their own purposes and in doing so they cursed people, good people, forever. Then they sat back laughing, imagining that their position was unassailable, but now I am back!

'The battle of three days and three nights on the eastern shores of the Red Sea was not the end; it was a beginning. Now, the souls of these evildoers, wherever they are, will find no rest. I will find them and I will kill them and, most of all, I will extinguish their life force forever and the Earth will breathe again.

'Know the truth and the truth shall set you free, as Christ said. Man does not return to dust. He returns to spirit, until he learns how to rip the lies of his masters from his very cells, and that you must do also.

'You are answerable to the Universe. You will love the Universe with all your strength and with all your might. You will trust It completely and utterly and you will have faith in It. Next, you are answerable to yourself, and that is all. Rip the lies from your flesh with the burning flame of passion and truth so that your cells renew themselves as they were meant to do, without decay, without death and without end.' She paused to draw breath, obviously made weary by her own passion, but her eyes still glittered with an inextinguishable fire.

'You are good,' she said finally. 'Most people strive to be good but their lives are cut cruelly short. I say to the people who have done this to them – to those who constructed this lie and poisoned people with it, for I know who they are, and where they are, and who they pretend to be; I know the faces that they show to people and I know their real faces – I say: from now on, peaceful sleep will be denied you. All living things will turn against you because of all the wickedness you have done. Trees will scratch you. Dogs will bite you. Insects will sting you, even the rocks will be disgusted by you and never afford you shelter and in the end, you will find even the air will resist entering your lungs, and even if it should then it will surely suffocate you. Oh yes, I am back!

'And as for you, my dear friend, heed my words. Free yourself and help others to free themselves if you can, and then be like me, free and without end.'

NECESSARY, FOREVER

NECESSARY, TO BURN OUT

FALSE SHAMES AND SMELT

THE HEAVIEST ORE OF THE BODY

INTO PURITY

D. H. Lawrence

# Chapter Ten

## *To sleep and dream of sheep*

'Sorry if I frightened you,' smiled Lilith, several nights later. 'I get carried away sometimes. Old angers and rages from history come flooding back to me and then I want to exact horrible vengeance on all evildoers. I've calmed down now, hence this scenario of the rich and cosy living room, which I believe to be quite in keeping with your century and your concept of what is normal. Don't blame me if it's wrong. All the images are drawn from your own subconscious memories, even down to the three porcelain flying ducks on the wall over there.'

'I do not have flying ducks in my unconscious mind!' I protested.

'Oh yes, you do,' she cooed mockingly. 'It's very primitive inside your unconscious mind, very bare and spartan.'

'I've been thinking,' I said, sighing deeply. 'I'm convinced that I'm quite insane. All I seem to do is to have crazy dreams about you every night, and that does make me question my sanity.'

'That's because of your TRIBALISTIC CONDITIONING,' she said, 'the eighth deadly venom.' She paused and smiled. 'You measure all your concepts in terms of how everyone around you thinks and it is very hard for you to step outside of those rigid boundaries.

155

Tell you what, I'll go and put the kettle on and we'll both have a nice cup of tea and a biscuit, and you'll feel much better. Insanity is only relative, after all, I mean, tell me one thing that you do that the people in your society don't do? Go on, think about it.'

'Well, they don't dream about you, for a start,' I observed.

'Well, of course not. I wouldn't be seen dead in most people's dreams. I mean apart from that, cretin.' I pondered the question for a long time, while Lilith yawned and patted her mouth, feigning extreme boredom and practising her patronising sigh, which she did awfully well. I realised too that the offer of tea and biscuits had also been a taunt drawn from my own unconscious mind.

'Can't think of anything,' I said finally.

'Precisely,' she exclaimed, 'because you're a sheep, baaaa! The shepherd says, "Go over there" so you go over there. The shepherd says, "Go into that pen with all the other sheep" and you do so. The shepherd says, "Come here, little sheep, and I'll put a bolt through your brain, cut you up and eat you" and you say, "Oh, thank you, good, kind shepherd". See? You're a sheep, baaaa!'

'I suppose you have a point,' I said rather lamely.

'I always have a point!' she snapped, 'I haven't wasted one single word since I was created, everything about me is pointed, accurate and true. Oh dear, you are the intellectual equivalent of wading through quicksand. Do try and see the bigger picture!'

'I suppose the question is,' I said, 'how does one escape these conditionings?'

'Logically that would seem to be the obvious question, but there is a more important question.'

'Which is?' I asked.

'Who is the shepherd?' she smiled. 'Or, to be more accurate, who are the shepherds?' I blinked with surprise. It was indeed an interesting and unexpected question.

She waved her hand and the living-room scenario vanished, to be replaced by a classroom. I suddenly found myself sitting at a seemingly tiny desk, in the front row, alone, while she stood dressed in a teacher's gown and mortarboard before a huge blackboard.

'Right! Pay attention,' she shouted in a high-pitched headmistressy voice. 'Remember this scenario? It was the first sheep-pen, and you all sat there, sucking in knowledge and never once questioning the origin or authenticity of anything you were told. So, now we will have a real lesson.' She produced some chalk from the air and glanced at it with some surprise.

'Hmm,' she murmured, 'my ability to materialise matter is improving.' Then she returned abruptly to the subject of her lesson.

'Very well. Now I'm going to proceed very fast in case I repeat myself from earlier lessons, but basically we can start with the destruction of the Matriarchal Age by the Chango people. So I'll write "Matriarchal Age" here, then the conquering barbarians – God rot their eyes – divide into city-states ruled over by cruel warlords. So I'll draw lots of lines indicating Chaldea, Mesopotamia and Ur.

'From that all roads lead to, first, the systematic subjugation of women, which of course altered their DNA programmings; and, second, the early formation of organised patriarchal power. In other words, the beginnings of what I have quaintly termed "the shepherds".' She drew a long sweeping line to the other side of the blackboard.

'I'll hurry through the Dark Ages and the Middle Ages. All cruelty, cruelty and yet more cruelty, how surprising! And the Renaissance, ignorance, ignorance and even more ignorance, makes me shudder to think about it – all the way up to your present day. Are you still with me?' I nodded and tried not to smile at the flamboyant way she flew through the centuries.

'So,' she went on enthusiastically, 'we can now deal with the various aspects in which sheep – I'm sorry, people – are controlled in your 21st century.' She vigorously wiped all her writings off the blackboard and wrote 'methods of control' in large letters as a heading.

'One,' she began, writing a large number one on the left-hand side of the blackboard and putting a circle around it. EDUCATION. Everything that is taught is censored history. Far from enlightening you, as it claims to do, it actually keeps you in perpetual ignorance because it never states or even alludes to the existence of controlling influences, let alone their motives.

'For example, children are not taught that millions of women and many, many kindly men were executed during the so-called witch-hunts, let alone by whom or given all the gory details of such executions. The fact that it was a blatant attempt to cull the power of women and their group consciousness is ignored. All outrages are essentially diluted or simply never mentioned, therefore the existence of organised evil is concealed from one's perceptions.

'Two, MEDICINE, fundamentally a slave of the pharmaceutical industry, which costs out diseases according to profit rather than cure, because if cures were readily available there would obviously be only a minimal need for drugs. Also, medical knowledge has always been under the control of a social elite who have drawn their knowledge not from a study of life but rather from a study of death, the dissection of dead bodies. Therefore, because of the elitism, new and progressive ideas have always been frustrated and accepted only when the appropriate profit motive had been introduced.

'Also, it is a fact that millions of, how do you say?, what is the word?, ah, prescriptions – thank you, I managed to find the energy signal pertaining to that word in your memory banks – yes, these are issued for mood-controlling drugs, tranquillisers, anti-depressants and the like, which dull the perceptions of people and make it impossible for them to think or reason or to question anything. If one is never made aware that this process is intentional then, again, the ordinary person does not perceive the existence of a controlling force lurking nastily behind the reason for formulating these chemicals in the first place.

'Three, MONEY, essentially another word for numbers. One must keep the populace affluent enough to function as slave sheep, yet poor enough to be distracted by worry, hence the constant encouragement to enter into states of impossible debt. This is achieved through the constant promotion and emphasis on credit cards, loans, mortgages and the like, because, once people have been tricked into existing in debt, then they can easily be controlled, whenever necessary, by the dubious manipulation of interest rates and the creation of artificial recessions.

'The term "money" has been cleverly equated over the centuries with the word "value", when, viewed dispassionately, money as such has no value at all. This can easily be proven by simple mathematics.

'For example, if we know the total wealth of the richest thousand people in just your country alone, and assume for a second that all this money is accruing interest, or, to use the correct derogatory word from your past as one should, usury, at the rate of ten per cent per annum, then the usury alone, in just one year, amounts to an enormous figure.

'Now where does this money come from in a national economy with a reported growth rate of less than four per cent? Answer, it comes from you, of course. You and people like you are actually getting poorer, because of the debt trap and because of your unawareness that paper money, which is supposedly a cheque that guarantees a fixed amount of gold, is no more than a fraudulent piece of paper, which actually guarantees nothing at all.

People have been tricked into believing that the paper itself has value, when of course it does not. The real power of control comes from the manipulation of this illusion.

She sighed deeply. 'I know you are exceeding your mental comfort zone,' she said, 'but events are shortening the space available for you to absorb this knowledge. The frequency of the air is rising, the frequency of the Earth is rising. Everyone on your world will be asking deep intelligent questions soon, and if you are to survive then you must be able to keep pace with your world's social evolution, and maybe even help certain people as well. So please try and bear with me, you can sleep any time, but you can't hear this any time. I will continue.

'Number four,' she said, enunciating slowly, obviously becoming weary with the role of teacher, 'is what is quaintly called on your world 'SEX', and she made a face, as if the prospect of talking about the subject disgusted her, which it did.

'You see, there are two evils here. First, the disgusting, repulsive, patriarchal warlords originated, and then their descendants promoted, a form of intimacy which, in an energetic sense, is essentially the wrong way round. Ideally, in a matriarchal world, men should feed women with energy on every level, sometimes practical, sometimes emotional and intimate, the latter taking the form of pleasure. Then the woman has reserves of energy with which to work her magic.

'In this exchange, the woman is energised and remains young and the man receives the energy of her approval and also stays young. The patriarchal way is basically for the man to conquer and dominate the woman and to feed from her energy, so she is poisoned and the man receives the energy of her contempt, which ages him, so they both die.

Good men and women still suffer, because after generations of conditioning they are only faintly aware of the existence of a different way, although women, being closer to the source than men, do often sense that there must surely be something better, for they hear echoes from their DNA and from the feminine group conciousness.

She placed her hands firmly on her hips. 'And then, of course,' she went on emphatically, 'there is the fact that those who organise your patriarchal society have consciously and deliberately, by means of the various forms of media, dragged the whole subject of intimacy down to the lowest possible level of degradation so that people caught up in the awful dynamic of it all have virtually no chance of raising their perceptions and only a small possibility of ever remembering how things should rightly be.'

'You're not happy with this subject, are you?' I commented.

'I certainly am not!' she retorted. 'I find lecturing on degradation very disconcerting, and there is one more very important point,' she continued, pointing a forefinger at me. 'They, them, those whose heads will end up on poles if I have my way with things, as if it wasn't bad enough to corrupt the whole of human relationships, they introduced their own twisted and perverted practices into your society in order to degrade people even further, and you know exactly what I mean!'

'I do,' I answered, 'but you're not accusing me of doing that, are you?'

She blinked in surprise. I always liked it when she did that, for it gave her an air of innocence and accentuated the beauty of her timeless eyes.

'Of course not! Why should you think such a thing?'

'Your finger,' I said 'It's pointing at me in an emphatic way.' She glanced at her finger, which was most elegant.

'Oh, that's just to emphasise a point. I use my eyes to accuse. Shall we move on?'

'I have a slight headache,' I said, which was true.

'Oh, dear, dear,' she mocked. 'Please do excuse me. I travel five hundred and eighty billion light-years to teach you things, and you get a headache. Well, remembering all that I've taught you, why do you have the headache?'

'I don't know,' I mumbled.

'Yes, you do.'

'Don't.'

'Yes, you bloody well do!' she shouted. 'Now spit it out.'

'Well,' I began hesitantly, 'I was worried that what you were talking about, er, was perhaps, um, in part, in me.'

'And why should you think that? Have you ever desired that?'

'No.'

'Then you don't need a headache in order to worry about it, do you!'

'No,' I smiled. 'I don't suppose I do.' And the headache instantly vanished.

'To move on, finally,' she said, clearly drawing on her reserves of patience. 'Number five, this is RELIGION. Religion thrives on preaching the duality of good and evil when in fact both are derived from the intentions and motives of human beings. By the way, bad intentions exist only in your world because that's where we put all you evolutionary dunces, to give you all so many "second chances" that we almost lose count of precisely how many chances you've all actually had.

'The so-called "holy books", which form the core of all religions, are composed of creeds written by brutal men for brutal men. Notice that I always distinguish between "brutal man" as the end-product of the barbarians and "civilised man" or "kindly man", who thinks and feels in a compassionate way. The latter group have always suffered with women throughout your history.

'People are led into the deadly trap of equating religion with goodness, when underlying religion, throughout your history, lie acts of such unspeakable horror that they make people like myself quite ill just to think about them, all driven by motives that have been so corrupt as to be frightening. But again, the controlling force and the people who govern it are both well hidden behind senseless and stupid rituals and dogmas, all designed to cloud the intellect.

'If science should ever replace such things as the modern religion, then that poses no problem to the forces of control. They will simply manipulate science as well and equate science with goodness also. They do not care what people believe so long as they are controlling it.

'The sixth subject is FOOD which is simply another control mechanism wrapped up in an attractive way to hide the fact that most of what people eat is poisonous to them. The human body and mind cannot function correctly if the DNA chain is incomplete. Hardly ever does a mother have the nutrition in her body to give birth to a child who has all the necessary minerals and supplements for a complete DNA.

'Therefore people remain dull-witted and their brains do not perceive or question as sharply as they should. This is obviously a useful control mechanism. I advise you to study in depth exactly what is put into food and how food is produced and exactly where food comes from. If you do that, I promise you, you will frantically try and produce your own, which is what you once did, but even then you were controlled by direct force and religion keeping you ignorant.

'You see, control mechanisms are like a wheel, which the bad shepherds can spin at any point in history; they can apply whichever mechanism is most effective for the social mood and climate. As one mechanism weakens, so another can be brought into play, while the preceding one is updated and modified, given a new disguise and made more effective, ready to be used again in the future.

'Seven. GOVERNMENT. This is simply the illusion of choice and the method by which opinions and principles are distracted by debate and rhetoric. The 'eternal sea'. As an objective student of the subject, the first thing you will note is the limitation of choice. In other words, you are essentially invited to choose the same product but in different wrappings. You are choosing the wrapping, not the product, which is how your life is managed. You are actually choosing who creates the most compelling illusion about the way your life should be managed, which gives you the illusion of having access to power and democracy when in reality you have no power whatsoever.

'All the strata of your life are placed beyond your control. Yet you are tricked into believing, first, that you choose the government you want in a free society and, second, even if you don't like it or agree with it, it is still essentially good for you, having been created by people who "know better" than you. Government is all about relentless and brutal global exploitation for the benefit of those in control. It is not about what is right or good for people and the sooner you realise this fact the better.

'The people who wield real dark power are all essentially invisible. They lurk in the machinery of applied government in which the visible leaders of political parties are selected figureheads for whichever wrapping you might wish to choose. The invisible ones laugh themselves senseless at the fact that you vote at all and imagine yourself to be making a choice, when in reality you are being fooled into approving the reinstatement of the same thing.

'Now, if you were allowed to choose the members of the Civil Service on the basis of disclosed ethics and beliefs and good deeds, that would be a different matter, but these people choose themselves. Remember the book 1984 by George Orwell, in which pornography was given a plastic coating to make people believe that they were obtaining something secret for themselves? And how this pornography was actually produced by computers, which randomly selected the various texts? It is the same thing, the rhetoric of the various political parties is the plastic coating, but the contents are always controlled and designed simply to distract you.

'Eight. NATIONALISM. This is the artificial creation of fear boundaries and barriers in the group consciousness of people and is one of the oldest control mechanisms. The moment that group consciousness moves upwards and people begin to think and to question the status quo, then a "war" is created, a conflict, a distraction. People are told all about "them", "over there", that "it" is all "their fault" and that "they" are a threat and are putting the populace in danger.

'Old hates are stirred up and fuelled. Situations are fabricated to provide evidence for the illusion. Scapegoats are found where necessary and forced through torture or blackmail to say that the illusion is real. War ensues, misery and suffering drag on for years and people never notice that the controllers of all this anguish are drawn from all sides, working all together, for their own benefit. The proof of this is that they are always still around at the end.

'War can also be extremely profitable, but its main power is that of distraction. The concept of nationalism appeals directly and ultimately to feelings of personal, family and social safety, which is why it is so effective when in truth, all families, from all parts of the world, simply want the same things – peace, progress and unity.

'Nine. TRANSPORT, the means by which the physical movement of people is monitored and, where necessary, restricted. You can drive your car anywhere you like provided that you are not challenging any of the control mechanisms. If you are, however, then all your movements can be monitored and your threat value evaluated. Have you not noticed the little cameras springing up everywhere above and beside the roads? Who do you think is really looking through them and why? Is an awareness of traffic flows really necessary at midnight? Think about it.

'You see, everything is designed to stop you thinking. Another useful aspect of transport – even the subject and the word seem so innocent, do they not? – is that it is a perfect excuse to destroy most of the natural environment. Firstly, it lowers the frequencies in the air by destroying trees, which filter the air, and by destroying animals, which breathe out pure air, and secondly, it makes people forget the reality of history.

'When you were a boy, on the hilltops were the gallows and the gibbets from which people were hanged, terrified out of their wits, until their brains seemed to explode with the inability to breathe, until they were forced petrified out of their bodies which then hung there and rotted, to frighten others into submission and to warn them of the consequences of disobedience. Where are those gallows and gibbets now I ask?

'They've all been taken down and probably sold to timber merchants, from where someone has bought them to make attractive beams for their period cottage – how's that for feng shui, then! But the people who hanged people and tortured them have not been removed. They are still here. They've just had a twenty-first-century makeover, that's all, and therefore history can be diluted even further until people completely forget what happened in the past and what was done, by whom and to whom. Oh yes, transport does have its uses!'

'Ten. EMPLOYMENT, a device that taps mainly into the male programming to provide for the family unit and everyone's fear of destitution. If work is made scarce and unpredictable and if everyone is constantly occupied in mostly pointless tasks, which make someone else rich, they will consequently have no time in which to reason their way out of the sheep-pen situation. It is essentially giving people something to do to stop them from thinking.

'The things that people are therefore given to do under the heading of "employment" usually fall into line, inevitably, with the perpetuation of a control mechanism. Thus, a teacher may unknowingly teach censored history, a doctor may unknowingly perpetuate the medical knowledge that was derived from dissection, a labourer may help to build a road through a forest and destroy the environment, all the while thinking he is benefiting society. All are feeding their families with the money they earn from their work, and all are being distracted.

'If human minds were free to function, people would very quickly realise what was going on. Therefore work and employment have to be perpetuated, even though employment is really just another word for ownership, which of course embodies the power of lifelong control.

'Eleven. LEISURE AND ENTERTAINMENT The purpose of these is to gradually dehumanise everyone by addressing their egos and by distracting them with illusions. Hence the suppression and financial neglect of the performing arts and the encouragement and ample funding of electronic leisure equipment.

'I tell you now, and pay close attention, your children are deliberately being re-programmed, on a DNA level, to accept and enjoy violence, brutality and obscenity by means of computer games so that when they are adults they will be more easily disposed towards these things and controlling them will therefore be much easier.

'This is one of the most sinister activities of your age. It has been slipped in, under everyone's nose, until now it seems almost mundane. By simply inserting a coin into a machine, a child can blow people to pieces in his mind when he is visiting an airport, a hotel, a restaurant, almost anywhere, in fact.

'The visual effects are subliminal and targeted towards his deep unconscious mind, in order to separate him from healthy imagination which he would achieve by reading a book, and to confuse his concepts of good and bad and of right and wrong. You see, children are naturally lazy. It is not their fault, but they will allow everything to be done for them until such time as they are activated into having a sense of responsibility towards others and an awareness of the needs of other people and a desire to assist them.

'This process of subliminal indoctrination is especially deadly because it influences them before they have formed the ability, through social interaction, to discern reality from illusion. If they, and indeed adults, saw the reality of treating gunshot wounds in the casualty unit of a hospital, they would be unable to classify the experience as an entertainment and would of course not wish to play a computer game woven around the subject.

'Children have always played at being soldiers and cowboys and Indians, but this has always been on a physical and imaginative level where all the rules of good personal conduct apply, and where honour and compassion can come into play. The computer game acts on an unconscious mental level only. Pain, touch and feelings are all abstracted. So just as the way to conquer an army is to divide it, so too if you divide feelings from intellect in the human mind, you can conquer and control that also and create a behavioural nightmare.

'Twelve, the MEDIA. Basically everything that is reported to you as news has been monitored and where necessary altered to protect and perpetuate the status quo. In your Middle Ages, for example, many months could elapse before the ordinary person, living in rural England, would be told that some important event had taken place. Now, in the present age on your world, "knowing something" is almost instantaneous. It is essential, therefore, to keep rigid control of what people know and how and when they know it.

'Even a journalist cannot access information that is not readily made available but a psychic can do so. The journalist can only perceive the consequences of an actual event rather than the event itself. For example, he can report the horrors of a conflict that he sees and about which the people involved tell him, but he cannot perceive that the conflict was deliberately induced for outside motives. He cannot perceive that both sides were supplied with weapons and ammunition by the same country using different companies, or that the crippling debt keeping that country in abject poverty has been deliberately created to hold back the social progress of that country.

'Even if the journalist does sense that something underhand is taking place, his or her editor, who will have to follow political guidelines, can easily censor the report. If these guidelines are not rigidly adhered to, then sanctions can be imposed upon the newspaper, radio or television station in the form of coverage deprivation and loss of funding.

'I hear the energy of your mind ask, "What about an earthquake, a tidal wave or a hurricane?". Well, the consequences of these are obvious, but one will never read or hear that such events happened because billions of gallons of oil have been pumped out of the Earth, thus disrupting all the energy meridians, or because the vibrational frequency of the air has become so negative and unstable that a natural and explosive reaction occurred.' She paused and took a long deep breath.

'Do you know,' she said finally, 'I'd forgotten just how boringly primitive existence is on your world. On my world I lecture on spatial politics, you know, not that you would understand it.'

'Try me,' I said, beginning to develop a serious headache, even though I was dreaming.

'Spatial politics is the subtle interaction of positive energies within a given situation to create maximum pleasure. It requires a great deal of very complex mathematics, which you wouldn't be able to comprehend. Anyway, I know you are bored and anxious to rest your brain but I do have to do this, so if you will please try and remain aware for just a little while longer it would be very much appreciated, thank you.

'Shepherds,' she went on, 'this is a gross blasphemy upon shepherds, because shepherds care for their sheep, but nevertheless, if shepherds will forgive me, I will continue to use the analogy. You and all good people must know who they are, and that is not easy because they camouflage themselves within all the complex machinery of society and government.

'As organisations, they have existed for a very long time, as I have already explained, so they have become very clever, very devious and very dangerous. The human race upon your world must seek them out, expose them and terminate them, the sooner the better, and then peace and reason will reign supreme. I feel you thinking, "How does the human race terminate them?" Well, once they are incarcerated, then the rising tide of awareness will do the job by making the air unbreathable to them.' She paused and took a long, deep breath.

'All the leaders of organised criminal syndicates must be eradicated. All members of the international masonic movement, the so-called "illuminati", must be terminated, and all religious people in high office who have dealings of any kind with the first two evil groups I have mentioned must be erased.

'Total focus must be placed upon the elimination of wrong and corrupt motives wherever they may be found. Obviously wrong motives occur in varying degrees of severity. Where these are relatively mild and correctable, then the instigators may be allowed to perpetuate their existence, after suitable rehabilitation, of course.

'If the wrong is extreme, regardless of allegiance to any organised group or not, the instigator must be thrown back into the state of non-existence. People on your world must question the structures that surround them and ceaselessly search for the truth in all things. Only then can the natural order of things be restored.' She folded her arms.

'This is the end of your lecture,' she said. 'Now you have ten minutes of uninterrupted sleep before the light from your sun-star streams in through your bedroom window and wakes you up – good morning!'

I awoke with a throbbing headache that persisted for most of the day, relenting slightly only towards late afternoon. It was a wet and windy Sunday, and I decided to go for a drive through the countryside to try and clear my head. Instead of lifting my spirits, however, the gloomy weather made me feel even more depressed as I dwelt upon all the sombre things that Lilith had told me.

So everything was controlled and corrupt, I thought, and most of the powerful people are bad. There was no point in trying to vote for change when my vote didn't matter anyway – everything seemed such a mess. Progress in society, if there was progress at all, seemed so painfully slow in coming.

I parked the car and walked to the top of a low hill, sat with my knees tucked under my chin, feeling thoroughly miserable as the daylight faded. Rain began to fall, but I didn't care. I might as well get soaked to the skin as well, I thought, even though I did feel rather stupid and self-indulgent at the same time.

From the corner of my eye I watched a police car go past on the road below. I saw the police driver, a young man of about thirty, looking up at me, but I didn't take any notice until some ten minutes later when he drove back, stopped his car in front of mine, got out and slowly strolled up the hill to join me.

'Anything wrong?' he asked, smiling.

'Everything is wrong,' I answered. 'The whole system is wrong.'

'Oh dear,' he said, sitting down beside me, 'another case of over-exposure to the tabloid press. Can you explain how, by getting soaking wet and probably catching pneumonia, you intend to change anything?'

'I'm just having a bad day,' I said pathetically.

'Girlfriend or wife problems, I expect,' he said, reaching into his tunic for a pack of cigarettes and a lighter. He offered me a cigarette, which I accepted, and he managed to light them both in the rain. 'What's her name?'

'Lilith,' I answered.

'Unusual name, what part of the world might she be from, then?' I simply stared blankly at him, not wishing to run the risk of being certified as insane if I chose to answer.

'She confuses me.'

'Oh, tell me about it,' he laughed. 'My wife confuses me something rotten but I love her to bits. Everything gets sorted eventually you know; you just have to give it time.'

'Look,' I said, 'you're very kind, and I know you're trained to spot potential suicides and crazy people, but I have no intention of ending it all. I'm not mad and I don't want to waste your valuable time.'

'So you're telling me politely to clear off, then?' he said.

'No, of course not. I wouldn't be that rude. It's just that I know that I look a bit odd, sat up here in the rain, contemplating the meaning of life, but I'm not in danger and I'm not a danger, that's all.'

'Never thought you were,' he shrugged. 'I just thought you looked a bit daft, that's all. I don't mean to be unkind, but I think you're being part of the problem rather than the solution.' I simply stared at him and he smiled back.

'Oh yes,' he went on happily. 'I know all about problem people, bad people. It is my job after all. I catch 'em if I can, and they end up behind bars eventually, even though of course they all think they're really clever and will never get caught, but they always do, in time.'

'But what about organised crime?' I asked. 'The really high-up, invisible people?'

'Bigger they come, the harder they fall,' he answered. 'You see, what these people forget is that the vast majority of people are good, and you can't exploit good people forever. Eventually society will clean up its act and everyone will be happy, in time. You tell your girlfriend that! With all due respect to her, maybe she thinks too much. She needs to have more fun, and get out and about more.' I started to smile. 'If he only knew,' I thought.

'And so do you, by the look of you,' he continued. 'Remember, only happy people change the world. The second that you let it all get you down, then you become part of the problem. I know what you're thinking, what about this and what about that – but people aren't stupid, you know, and they're getting smarter all the time, they're not a load of sheep any more!'

'Well, thank you,' I said. 'You're very wise.'

'No,' he smiled, 'I just know that if bad was stronger than good, then you and I wouldn't be here talking now. This world of ours would be long gone.'

He stood up and tried to wipe the water from his tunic. 'Now I'm going to go home,' he said, 'hang all this up to dry, have my dinner, then get into a nice hot bath, jump into bed and sleep.'

'And dream of sheep?' I asked humorously. He simply smiled and ambled back down the hill towards his car.

TELL HIM TO LIVE BY

YES AND NO –

YES TO EVERYTHING GOOD

NO TO EVERYTHING BAD

William James

# Chapter Eleven

## *And straight on till morning*

By now the world of dreams and visions and teachings had become my real world, and I merely paid lip service to the mundane world which most people regarded as the ultimate form of reality. I knew that I was part of something different and higher than normal existence, but although this all seemed very grand and brought great rewards in the form of insights, it also carried greater penalties for ignorance, wrong-doing or lack of awareness. I accepted that, in my own small way, I was working for the Universe now, like a humble clerk working within some vast multinational corporation.

I sensed that everyone had a routine inflicted upon them as soon as their childhood was over, and with it playtime and school. Almost immediately after the demise of these brief periods of joy and innocence in their lives, 'grown-up' people told them what the 'real' world was all about, the so-called 'facts of life', and before they could even think, they were thrust into the world of mortgages, relationships, bills and commitments, always being told that this was the only good and right way in which to live. So of course this all quickly took them over and became their unquestioned routine. Yet often, I suspected, in the small hours of the night whenever sleep might be elusive, they would wonder, 'Is this all there is?'

The adult world that I had entered into had been very simple. Hard work provided social acceptability and created money which bought food to eat and clothes to wear and the right to live in a house, by paying rent or a mortgage, thereby securing warmth and shelter and the abstract sense of respectability. The doctor or, in extreme cases, the hospital took care of your health. The dentist maintained your teeth. Police made sure that everything was peaceful. You would employ a lawyer perhaps once or twice in a lifetime to deal with important legal issues, and a priest who represented the church dealt with the vast world of the unknown.

All belief systems were 'off the peg' and passed on to you as soon as you left school, rather like a soldier being issued with his kit, and then 'real' life began and playtime was most definitely over.

The sad thing about it all was that everyone, regardless of social status, seemed caught up in this system of routine. The doctor and the dentist, the lawyer and the policeman all had the same problems as we had. They all grew old and tired, they just lived in a better house and had rather more money than we had to spend on luxuries, but even as a child I realised that no-one escaped the routine.

This was often conveyed as the concept of 'law and order', rather than 'routine', and seemed on the surface to be very commendable. I could not understand, however, why everyone trapped within it suffered hurt so much and achieved happiness in short bursts, before succumbing to some illness or problem and then becoming old, following the dictates of routine into the idea of 'retirement' and then eventually dying.

Whenever I happened to wander around a cemetery, as one does sometimes when exploring old churches, I realised that everyone who was laid to rest there had had hopes and dreams, loved and laughed and cried, just like me, and they had all suffered the same fate. There had to be so much more, which people did not know. They obviously hadn't known enough to be able to save themselves. Then I felt rather arrogant and judgmental, yet it seemed an inescapable fact that 'off the peg' beliefs certainly did not work for people.

They did not work because they were contrived. They had been conceived and created for people to live inside them, never knowing that there was anything different. Lilith was right, people were always distracted – by debts, the threat of unemployment, the possibility of illness or, on a much bigger scale, by some national upheaval or the threat of war. They only had enough time in which to work, eat and sleep, never any time to think. The question then was – had people organised themselves in this way? Was this how they really wanted it? Or had it all been orchestrated around them in order to keep them in ignorance? I suspected the latter, as Lilith had expressed it to me.

Some subtle trick was being played on people; the giveaway was the fact that the moment one questioned the foundations of secular or temporal authority, one was labelled as 'bad' or 'troublesome', even though the questions were valid enough. I could ask a priest a question and his answer would be based on his knowledge of the Bible. If I dared to question the Bible, then I was deemed to be anti-social and placed on the fringes of the society, which functioned through blind routines.

If I questioned a doctor, whose knowledge was founded in a system of Western medicine that had drawn its understanding of physiology from the dissection of dead bodies then, again, I was being 'offensive' and 'difficult'. I was never allowed to access the real person beneath the role that they had chosen to play within the social system. If priests had crises of faith they kept them

179

strictly to themselves. How did doctors feel when their patients died? Difficult questions were almost always dealt with by ostracising the questioner.

It was very painful to me to realise that all the people who had influenced me – my brilliant teachers, Jane and all the others who had pointed the way through the jungle of life – must be suffering from pollution by now. Jane was probably married, with children. Her face would be lined, her skin would be sallow and she would probably have lost her charming vitality. Some others would certainly be dead by now, or very feeble, living out their days in some residential home.

None of them would have survived in a quality way. Not one of these magnificent people would have escaped the traps. It broke my heart to think of Mr Packer or Mr Ricketts waiting out their last days, staring through some curtained window at the memories from their lives and being tended by hard-pressed nurses who simply did not have the time to love them.

Lilith was right. Something or someone was murdering people, and finding out who the culprits were must be the last piece of the riddle.

When I next dreamt of Lilith she was seated on a white throne in the vast room of a palace. All around the walls were statues of people whom I could not identify. The floor was formed of deep blue hexagonal crystals. The ceiling was of deep blue, scattered with glittering jewels like stars. She sat resplendent in a red velvet cloak. Upon her head she wore a fabulous crown of gold bearing the symbols of the owl, the eagle, the lion and the dragon, and it was decorated with beautiful feathers, which hung down over her long hair.

In her left hand she carried a sword and in her right hand she held a sceptre, and on either side of the throne there was a fountain in which crystal clear water rose up and splashed and glittered. Behind the throne was a window through which I could see a billion stars and the palace seemed lit by an inner light, a soft peaceful light, which was very hypnotic.

'Greetings, old friend,' she said, 'we have come a long, long way together, down so many centuries, and now at last you can see me as I really am.' She paused and smiled. 'This is my home,' she said, gesturing around her with the sceptre. 'Everything is pure and perfectly clean, and most of all, eternal.' She smiled again, sensing that I was trying to work out what everything meant.

'This palace is where I view your world,' she said. 'I have created it with my feelings. Everyone creates their surroundings with their feelings, even people in your world. You should know that by now. The statues are not dead figures of stone, because nothing is dead. They are watchers, and they see anything that I do not see, and I can place my hands upon them and their energies will tell me all that they have seen and learnt. The floor bears the energy and therefore the colour of pure femininity. The ceiling reminds me of the vast Universe. My cloak represents blood, the life force, dynamic power, and the crown marks me out as a queen.

'The owl is wisdom gleaned from the beginning of ages. The eagle transcends everything and sees everything. The lion has the strength to endure the pain of the failings of others and the dragon links me with the arteries of the Earth. The feathers symbolise flight and freedom. The sword is justice, bringing release for the good and misery for the bad, and the sceptre, with all its symbols and carvings, represents the power of woman. It was a present to me given by the first man ever to walk this world.

'Through my window I can watch starships travelling the deep reaches of the Universe, and from this throne I can communicate with my friends who live on far-distant worlds. I sit and I wait, I wander the rooms of this palace, longing for the day when humanity will evolve into full conscious awareness.'

'I am feeling very sad,' I said, 'and I don't exactly know why.'

'I know,' she answered, making a sad face at me. 'It's because soon we must part, and you will dream of me no more.'

'I don't think I can bear that,' I said with difficulty.

'Oh, but you must,' she implored me. 'You have work to do. Then you must reach me through your own efforts. Conquer your fears, live by your awareness of things, and you will grow ever closer to me.' She held out her arms to me.

'Remember,' she said slowly, 'remember, you have been here before; blood-stained and terrified. You stood almost on the very spot you are standing now and said, panting with exhaustion, "The Chango are but fifty miles from us, my queen, and they come quickly." I said, "Very well, now go and join the escort army, help lead my priestesses to safety, immediately." You pleaded with me to be allowed to stay, but I ordered you to go. Now it is the same, only with a bright future ahead of us.'

'But I want to stay in your world,' I protested.

'You have not yet earned the right,' she answered. 'If I stay close to you, then your energies will kill me. The frequency of your cells is much lower than my own. Our energies are incompatible. I would be brought down to your level and that is why I have always come to you in dreams and never openly. So you must work on yourself, so that we can meet without me being polluted.

'But we are not yet finished with this encounter. There is still one more deadly venom, the most deadly of all, and you must understand it completely.

'Remember what you were told about the matrix? People must understand in your world that they affect everything around themselves by their own energy emanations – humans, animals, plants, the atmosphere and the Earth itself. At the moment they have created a matrix of darkness, ignorance and selfishness as they struggle to live within it, but as soon as they realise that their reality depends on their own emanations and their own motives, and once they have learnt kindness and compassion and the art of true selfless giving, then the matrix in which they dwell will change and they will perceive a higher form of reality.'

'Yes, I understand,' I said, 'but what is the last deadly venom? Please tell me.'

'HUMAN BREATH,' she answered.

'You mean, people kill one another?'

'Of course, you know they do. Even they know they do, but they'll never admit it. They breathe their hate and resentment and greed and treachery into the faces of others. The negative energy gets inside everyone's lungs, then into their bloodstreams, and then into what you call their DNA, and it changes them, lowers their cellular frequencies, leaving them open to disease and decay. It kills animals and plants and trees. It gets blown about by the wind and eventually affects life forms all over the world.

'Think about it, a large city in your world, with a population of maybe eight million people. Let us assume that seventy per cent of them are relatively unevolved. So, we have five point six million pairs of lungs, breathing at a rate of ten to fifteen times a minute. Multiply the average lung capacity by two, and then by ten or fifteen, and then by sixty, for there are sixty minutes in one hour, and then by twenty-four, since there are twenty-four hours in one of your days. Multiply again by three hundred and sixty-five, for that is the number of days in a year, and then by five point six million, and you have the volume of negative breath energy that is released into the air by the inhabitants of just one of your cities in one year. Frightening, isn't it?

'You see, the battle between good and evil takes place in the air. High-frequency breath against low-frequency, poisonous breath. That's why we allow animals and plants to suffer in your world, because animals breathe out pure air and plants filter negative energy from the air. Without them you would all suffocate through your own negativity.'

I became very despondent and shook my head sadly. 'There is no hope for people, is there? I mean, any fool can see that the way they behave is wrong but they just don't seem to care. It is all such a mess.'

'Yes, it is. But to make the subject easier to understand, you must divide people into three groups. First, you have good people who are always trying to better themselves; people who are kind and acutely aware of life around them. These people breathe out high-frequency energy, which enhances and helps to heal everything it touches, and those who observe the progress of this world honour these people.

'The second group is very large. It comprises spirits who are neither good nor bad. They simply allow others to do the work of change for them. They are lazy and mean and their minds are closed. They do not even think globally, let alone universally, and their breath makes no difference at all, it is simply neutral.

'Last, of course, we have people who enjoy being wicked, who like hurting people and animals, and who delight in destroying all things natural, good and wholesome. They know that they spread misery, pain and suffering all around themselves, but they simply do not care. They are quite contemptuous of the sufferings of others, and their breath is foul, low-frequency poison.

'Because of its high atomic weight it hangs close to the ground and hampers the work of good people and tends to make a person in the "neutral" category more likely to become bad. So, although the air separates according to its frequencies, socially in your world, all three types of people are mixed together creating, as you rightly say, a mess.

'It is also important to realise that the extremely bad people throughout your history have always organised themselves into secret societies and brotherhoods, in order to make themselves stronger and to concentrate their wicked energies. So, as I've told you before, it has been and is very hard for the ordinary person to realise exactly what is going on, and even harder for them to change the situation. The wicked people always make sure that good people are confounded and confused at every turn. Always pretending, of course, that organised wickedness does not exist.'

'What will happen to these wicked people?' I asked. 'And who are they?'

'Do you wish to make me angry!' she smiled. 'I am not quite so beautiful when I'm angry. My face tightens and seems hard, my cheekbones become over-accentuated, but then, maybe even then, I am just as beautiful. I apologise, but when I think of them and of what I wish to do with them, I am consumed with an inner rage. Come, walk with me through the gardens of this palace, take the air with me.'

The gardens were indeed beautiful. We passed through a white marble archway to emerge surrounded by trees and flowers of every colour and variety, set around miniature lakes bedecked with fountains and statues.

'The sun has come out!' I exclaimed. 'How amazing.'

'Yes,' she smiled, 'I felt it ought to be so, and it was so. Don't you think I'm amazing?'

'I always have,' I answered, and she laughed politely.

'Everything has to breathe,' she went on. 'Evil people have always tried to make the air foul so that they might feel more comfortable. This is why they all cling together in groups, to create and share the same bad air. This is also why brutal man has always delighted in slaughtering animals, millions of animals of every species, and continues to do so, because he knows that animals breathe out pure air which is offensive to them.

'Driven by the same motive they try to destroy the forests, again to make the air more to their liking. As for who they are, everyone knows in their heart whether they do good things or bad. Those who know that they do bad things and do not care, they will be the ones to perish by my hand.'

She paused and sat demurely upon an ornate wooden chair, the back of which was intricately carved with designs depicting birds of paradise.

'The solution is to discipline and to be disciplined,' she said. 'People must realise that they are not isolated beings and that they affect everything around themselves with their emanations. So they should not be so selfish. Rather they should look around and see who or what needs their help. If they see injustice, they must oppose it and say, "No, this is dangerous and damaging and wrong. You, the instigator, must stop, you will not be tolerated any more". That way, positive beautiful energy flows around and around, backwards and forwards, and everyone bathes in it and breathes it in and out, but no-one must be allowed to spoil the innocent beauty of others, not one single person.

'To exact discipline requires toughness, courage and stamina, and it is anything but weak. It is fashionable to think of good as insipid and bad as somehow exciting and desirable but I tell you, until people stop playing victims and villains, there will be no peace on your good Earth.'

There was a fountain beside her and a butterfly was floundering in the water. She reached out and delicately lifted it free on the tip of her finger before blowing on its wings to dry them.

'You see,' she said, 'there was something close to me that needed me, in one moment of time and space. That particular moment will never come again in the whole of forever. It called to me with its energy. It was terrified; it thought it was going to die, but now it is happy. It is just as beautiful as I, and now it can go about its business.' She blew lightly on the insect once more and it fluttered away, high over the nearby trees.

'Now it will be my friend forever,' she said, 'because it has absorbed my energy. As you would say, its DNA has recorded me, and that group consciousness will tell all other butterflies about me as well, and they too will become my friends but, of course, the opposite is also true!' She smiled wickedly and waved her hands before her face and instantly the scene changed.

We were suddenly standing in the steaming street of some dark city. Police-car sirens wailed and gangs of youths were wandering around, cursing and swearing and spitting. On one street corner, two young men were fighting, punching and kicking each other viciously. They were both bleeding profusely from face wounds and obviously doing frightening damage to one another. On another corner stood a group of drunken men who were shouting abuse at everyone. Another man was urinating against a shop doorway. There was a burnt-out car close to us and another car, without its wheels, which had obviously been stripped of all its valuable parts and was resting on piles of bricks.

Lilith was wearing her usual clothes again, black trousers and jacket, black top and black boots. Her clothes always seemed so well cut and extremely expensive. I had often wondered where she bought them or obtained them, and on which world!

'Welcome to goblin city,' she smiled. 'Everyone around you is using less than one per cent of their brains. They are afraid of everything, which is why they perceive everything to be a threat and attack everything and everyone – nice, isn't it!'

'I feel sick,' I said.

'I'm not surprised,' she answered. 'I would feel sick, too, were I not a highly evolved being able to shield myself from such base energies but even I cannot linger here for too long. I just wanted you to see how the other half live, as you would say.'

'I think we should leave,' I said fearfully. 'We're liable to get attacked at any moment.'

'Oh ye of little faith,' she said. 'I could eat this lot for breakfast – dear me, your base verbal expressions are quite infectious. I meant to say, I would be well able to defeat them all, had I the desire to do so, which I haven't. Anyway, they can't even see us. Our cellular frequencies are so high and theirs are so low that we are well outside of their visible spectrums. We are quite invisible to them.'

'What is the point of this?' I asked nervously.

'The point, dear boy, is simply to illustrate just how poisonous human breath can be. All these things, I hesitate to call them people, are breathing, unfortunately, and their breath is entering the Earth's atmosphere and poisoning everything with which it comes into contact. If anyone who is good should come near people like this, then their lungs would be filled with foul air and the base energies would very quickly enter their bloodstream, and then their DNA, and eventually kill them. It is an object lesson in just how serious this subject is.'

'And of course these people are everywhere,' I added.

'Absolutely everywhere, but only on this world; we keep all the scum in one place. Your towns and cities are full of them, and they drag higher people down, make them miserable, and they constantly work against the progress of civilisation.'

'So what happens to them?' I asked.

'Nearly all of them are spiritually dead,' she answered. 'Their cellular frequencies have become flatline, in fact, sometimes we refer to them as 'flatliners'. So when their hearts stop beating, then that's it. They cease to exist on any level. Of course, many highly evolved people work to minimise the damage that they cause while they are waiting to die, and sometimes we have to terminate them, for the common good, you understand.'

'Of course,' I said, feeling extremely nervous by now.

'If a person,' she went on, 'who is free of karma and who wishes to make progress and move on and up through the Universe is to have any hope of success he must exclude goblins from his life by any means possible, even those who are related to him, even those who purport to love him; and then he must associate with high-frequency people only. Doing this can be hard. It requires a lot of social courage but it has to be done.

'These are the obvious goblins, of course. It is the more subtle ones that the normal person has to guard against, those who dress well and seem quite intelligent, yet hide a mess of corrupt motives beneath their smiling faces.

Every family has such a person or persons somewhere.'
She paused and then said, 'Would you like to see?'

'Do I have a choice?' I asked.

'No.' she smiled. She waved her hand once more and
the scene changed to the living room of a quite well-to-do
family. The furniture and carpets were tasteful and
expensive and everything seemed much more civilised,
so much so that I breathed a long, deep sigh of relief.

Three children were seated around a large table,
apparently busy with schoolwork. There was an old lady
sitting in an armchair watching television, a man sat
opposite her reading a newspaper, and from the kitchen
came the clatter of cooking utensils, which I presumed
indicated that the lady of the house was preparing the
evening meal.

'It all looks so cosy, doesn't it?' observed Lilith
sardonically. 'Everyone is so happy and content and
normal – but wait, all is not as it seems!'

'Don't tell me,' I said cockily. 'They're all aliens,
cunningly disguised as humans.' She simply glared at
me.

'If you attempt a joke like that once more, I will hurt
you,' she said. 'This is not a game, it is deadly serious and
you must learn the way of such things otherwise you will
let me down. I am your teacher, after all, and if you let me
down I will hurt you even more.

'Also, I would have you know that some of my friends
are of the opinion that I am wasting my time attempting
to teach you anything. If they should be proved right and
laugh at me and say "told you so", then I will hurt you so
much that it will create a whole new concept of pain for
you, so shut up and listen.

'The only people with pure motives in this scenario,'
she continued, 'are two of the children and the woman in
the kitchen. The old lady is consumed with past

resentments and hates and disapproves of everyone. She uses subtle intimidation to draw energy from everyone. She will die, of course, because she is poisoning herself with her own negative energy.

'The man hates his wife and is actually having an affair with his secretary. So his breath poisons the wife and when he sleeps with her he poisons her even more, and of course the energy of his smouldering frustrations affects everyone. One of the children is an angry, lazy, unevolved spirit, cunningly disguised as a child. He disrupts everything that he can, feigns illness when he needs attention, which he does all of the time, and is always plotting and scheming in his little brain to make everyone else look bad.

'The other boy and the girl are being affected by his breath and have become very frightened of him. As for the poor woman in the kitchen, not only does she have to serve all of them, but also she is being poisoned by three of the people in this room and, worst of all, she doesn't have the faintest idea of what is going on. So she will gradually become ill, depressed and neurotic. She will age quickly, then eventually be put into a home for old people where she will die. So you see, this is a mess, and no-one will survive it.'

'Can't the woman take the two good children and just run away?' I suggested.

'But she doesn't realise that there is anything to run from,' said Lilith. 'You are so obtuse and tiresome at times. Don't you see, they tell her that it's all her fault, for being weak, inadequate and useless and she believes them. Anyway, how can she run with just two children? She can't see spiritual energy and even if she could, then society would slay her for leaving one child behind. "Bad mother", they would say, "guilty", "stone her".' She took a long, deep breath.

'What is needed here is truth and total honesty but it will be a long time coming, if at all. Even if it did, I doubt if it would be in time to save anyone.'

'Can't you do something?' I suggested.

'Not my job,' she answered curtly, making a face at me.

'Please,' I insisted plaintively.

'Oh, come on,' she snapped. 'This is a typical average family. If I sort this mess out then I might as well sort them all out and have to spend the next thousand years doing it. I do have a life of my own, you know.' She paused and looked at me. 'Oh, very well,' she said, and we moved into the kitchen where the woman was laboriously making pastry. Lilith tapped her on the shoulder and the woman turned around with a start and screamed with alarm.

'Oh, do shut up!' said Lilith. 'Look, the evolutionary gap between you and me is so great as to be almost unmeasurable.' The woman just trembled and stared at Lilith open-mouthed. 'My list of titles is so long, your puny brain simply couldn't comprehend them all so forgive me if I don't introduce myself. My overly compassionate friend here has taken pity on you, therefore I want to say some things to you and I will say them only once, so just listen.'

'You are all heart,' I said.

'And you can shut up as well,' she added.

'If you don't leave I'll call the police!' stammered the woman in terror. 'George! George! Get in here now. There's a weird woman in the kitchen and a burglar!' Lilith slapped her lightly across the face.

'How dare you,' she snarled. 'Me, weird, you unevolved moron. Anyway, I am the police, you fool. George can't help you, he's pretending to be an intellectual, now just listen.' The woman simply stared at her.

'Your husband, er, George, is ...,' she snapped her fingers trying to think of the common expression, and looked to me for the answer.

'Carrying on with his secretary,' I said.

Lilith made a face. 'How gross,' she said, 'but nevertheless, it will suffice; and he's been doing this for five years, so I suggest that you make plans to either get rid of him or to leave. If you don't, his energies will make you old and kill you. The wrinkled old crone in the corner – your mother, I believe – hates the sight of you and constantly strives to make your life a misery, so get rid of her as well. Your son, Peter, is the reincarnation of a freemason, and he'll bring you nothing but pain and misery unless you discipline his wicked spirit. So set to and make some changes. Take plenty of salt baths, face your fears, work through them and you might just survive.' She paused and glared at me. 'Will that do?' she asked.

'I am moved by your compassion and tactful understanding,' I said. Lilith snorted contemptuously and prodded the woman in the chest.

'Do you understand all that I have said?' she asked. The woman simply nodded vigorously, unable to speak.

'Good.' Lilith turned away. 'Sometimes,' she added, speaking to me, 'you have to slap them around a bit to make them understand.'

She snapped her fingers and there was a new scenario. A cosy flat, in which an apparently loving couple were cuddled together on a deep, comfortable red sofa. They were both watching television and eating snack food. Lilith and I were standing behind the sofa.

'And what's wrong with this arrangement,' I asked, 'apart from the dreadful television programme?'

'Oh, it all looks innocent enough,' said Lilith, 'except that both people have failed to perceive the shape of things to come. You see, the man believes that the woman loves him for who and what he is, when actually she merely wants him because of his future earning potential. The woman believes, for her part, that she is the only woman that he views in a sexual way, whereas actually he views every attractive woman in a sexual way.

'When they eventually marry and have children, the stress and pressure of trying to cope with life and looking after needy babies will expose their false motives and they will fight. They will each blame the other for lying from the start and for failing to understand the other, and they will separate. They are lazy spirits, you see, untested, therefore they will not be able to handle trouble which comes from dishonesty born of fear and ignorance.'

'And are you going to slap them around as well,' I asked, 'and frighten the wits out of them?'

'Oh no,' she smiled, 'they'll do that all by themselves!'

She waved her hand and we found ourselves sitting in the window seat of a café, looking out on to a busy street. Lilith was noisily drinking a chocolate milkshake through two straws, and I found that a cup of tea had somehow appeared in front of me.

'Would you like a biscuit,' she asked, 'or a piece of cake? I found that desire in the deep recesses of your mind. Cakes and biscuits are security items for you, are they not?' I simply smiled.

'I only brought you here,' she said, 'to watch all the polluted people go by. All of them struggling along, their bodies saturated in other people's low-frequency energies or even energy generated by themselves. Makes one wonder sometimes how they manage to stay alive for as long as they do.'

'I understand the message, the lesson,' I said.

'I know,' she smiled, pushing her empty glass to one side. 'Considering that you are a fear-filled emotional cripple, using a tiny proportion of your brain, I hate to admit it, but you have done rather well.'

I felt chills go through me, from the base of my spine to the back of my neck, and I suddenly became very nervous at the finality in her words.

'Now look,' she continued fondly, 'I don't want you to get all emotional, and start blubbering, because that sort of thing really embarrasses me – but I have to go home now.'

'You mean,' I said hesitantly, trying to be as brave as I could, 'that I won't see you again?'

'That is up to you,' she said. 'From now on you will do a great deal of work and if you face your fears, eliminate your negative aspects as much as you can and endeavour to raise your cellular frequencies constantly, then you can see me again. But if you are lazy or get side-tracked by silly thoughts and ideas, then you won't.' I could feel the beginnings of tears but I managed to control myself.

'And how long will that take?' I asked.

'That is entirely up to you,' she smiled kindly, 'but I am homesick now and I have friends whom I have neglected and I have work to do. Oh yes, I do work! I want to see my rooms again and have my familiar things around me.'

'You mean the palace that I saw?' I asked.

'Oh no,' she smiled. 'That was just one aspect of my past; something that exists in one frame of my age and space. It is like a memory that I can return to. One day, you'll be able to return to your memories as well. No, I mean the home where I live now.'

'And where is that?' I noticed that my tea was cold.

She gazed plaintively through the café window. 'A long, long way from here,' she said wistfully. 'Farther than you can imagine. Now, that genuinely isn't an insult.

It just really is a very long way away.' She reached out and placed her hand over mine.

'Be good,' she said. 'Most of all be bold and brave and true to yourself – and make me proud of you.' She stood up, still looking at me, 'Now look away and do not look back. Au revoir!'

I woke up crying my eyes out and I cried for days. Sometimes I still cry.

* * *

Ordinary people came back into my life and gradually my social life, indeed all aspects of my life, improved. I became more confident and accomplished and I began first counselling people and then, when I felt brave enough, I began to heal them. The magnitude and intensity of the work increased until I became a very good healer, good enough to allow myself the title of shaman.

When troubles come into our lives, in the guises of pain, grief or fear, it is important to realise that the thing we dread most is the state of not knowing what to do. Also troubles always seem to come at the most frightening and unexpected times and are always magnified in the small hours of the night, when we might look out from our windows at all the lights of our particular town or city and realise just how little help is actually out there.

The first thing to know is who we truly are, and if we are normal, well-meaning people, then we are all shamans. 'Shaman' is just a word for someone who changes something bad into something good or who creates something good, and you do those things. Every time you cook a meal or clean a house or earn a living to feed your family or relate to anyone in a meaningful way, provided it is done with a good heart, then you too are a shaman. There is no mystique about it and no elitism.

Power is simply knowing really useful things and either un-learning or not bothering to know things that do not work. That is the first thing to know, and all the rest is a journey of discovery into the real world of true feelings. Power over your life, your body and your future will stop you crying, and it will ease your fears. If you have lost someone dear to you, then such power will give you the courage to close the gap between what you know and what you don't know. In that which we 'don't know' lies great beauty and mystery, I promise.

There is not a heartbeat to lose – begin the journey now. I know that sometimes you are tired and afraid but you are most certainly alive. If you are alive you can feel and think and start exploring all the ways in which you can remove from your life all the things you do not want, starting with those ideas or concepts that you hold on to and that do not work.

The less useless baggage that you carry, the lighter and faster you will travel. You will travel to a place where there are no tears, no sickness, no guilt, no fear and no pain, but you must start now, for the good Earth is turning, ever turning, the sky is ever changing, and you must not waste one moment. Begin and your resolve will grow with each new discovery until your spirit positively flies, back to beauty and innocence.

There is no time for you to doubt your sacred origins or to put yourself down any more or to wander aimlessly lost in the dark forests of intellectualism and cynicism, for cynicism is just another way of expressing hurt. Who hurt you, and when, and why? Whose negative energy are you perpetuating?

While you have been reading these last few paragraphs, you have taken thirty more breaths, your heart has been beating and everything has changed. The Earth has moved, the planets and the stars have all moved. They call to you. Your destiny calls you to be like Peter Pan and to fly ever onwards and upwards, towards the second star on the right, and straight on till morning.

With optimism for a brighter future for everyone,

Alex Gordon

October 9th, 2004

# Appendix 1

**The true nature of Lilith – an answer to Patriarchal Age propaganda**
The central "character" in Nine Deadly Venoms is called Lilith. It's Lilith who reveals the Nine Deadly Venoms. A simple search on the Internet will reveal much conflicting information about Lilith. Unfortunately a lot of this information is derogatory and wholly inaccurate. What is written about Lilith is Patriarchal Age propaganda designed to push people farther and farther away from any true memory of the Matriarchal Age. Alex Gordon attempts to put the record straight.

**The true nature of Lilith by Alex Gordon**
Following the downfall of the Matriarchal Age the conquering barbarians destroyed nearly all remains of that age, and all references to feminine principles were either corrupted or demonised.

Over time, 'Astarte', the feminine principle of the Babylonians, became 'Astoreth', a new 'name' containing the vowels of the word 'boshet' meaning 'worthless' or 'unclean', thus, by speaking the name Astoreth people were actually blaspheming it. Likewise, 'Anu' the Celtic sky-goddess, degenerated in myth and folklore to become 'Black Annis', a repulsive old crone who lived in the Dane Hills of Leicestershire and who ate children. Such is the nature of propaganda.

The references to Lilith that are available refer to her as the rebellious first wife of Adam before Eve, and in biblical references or Hebrew legend as a 'night monster' or 'night hag' who spawns demons and, again, eats children. Even the name itself is a corruption, because the word 'lil' in Hebrew means 'demon' although in Sufi tradition it is stated that the name has an ancient Semitic root meaning 'night'. Also in Sufi tradition, because the old Akkadian form of her name was 'Lilitu', which in Hebrew becomes Lilith, the Arabic form becomes 'Layla', and to Sufis, Layla means the power of love, so at least they have retained some respect and correctness towards her true nature.

Now, the wheel of time has almost turned full circle. For thousands of years, the wind has blown over desert sands. The stars have journeyed across the heavens. The face of the Earth has reformed and been reshaped. Empires, kings, emperors have all come and gone, back to dust, until now,when, many billions of light-years away beyond the belt of Orion, a ship is coming. **It is a huge inter-galactic ship, black and powerful, and it is bringing Lilith back to re-establish the new Matriarchal Order.**

How do I know this? I can sense it, feel it. I know her energy. I know her, as much as my limited perceptions can do so and the sense of her ship droning through the vast expanse of deep space coming ever closer towards this planet gives me a deep sense of peace and reassurance, a feeling that I can, at last, rest.

**But what is she truly like?** This is a very hard question because truth can only be conveyed correctly to the limit of the reporter's perceptions and level of evolution. A good person will always see the good in things and find light and colour in their observations even though the amount of such brightness may be small. Conversely, a bad person will see the bad in everything and report that everything is bad. Therefore I cannot tell you the total truth, because I am not evolved enough to know that.

I believe her to be at least 280 million years old, and in that time she has obviously experienced and observed almost everything whereas I, by comparison, have observed and understood virtually nothing. I do not know and cannot even begin to understand where or how she was born or where she lives or the manner of her life, although I believe that she lives much as we do except that in her world there is no negativity, a state of which we can barely imagine.

**I know her to be incredibly beautiful, wise, vain and tempestuous yet clinically efficient. I suspect her to be rather insular and private and to communicate with pure feelings. I believe also that she can alter and form matter with thought.**

When anyone searches for her, the information will fall into four categories. Firstly, the old legends formed from barbaric propaganda which simply insult her and which come in many diverse forms but which are all basically blasphemous towards her. Secondly, her name and image has become something of a feminist icon, which is understandable given the nature of the legend that she was Adam's first rebellious wife, but this too is completely misplaced because although, yes, she is a woman, she is not like women here simply because she is using so much more of her DNA and also has so many more references in her DNA.

The idea that she should need or wish to be a 'feminist' is quite laughable, given that I feel certain that she could destroy any enemy with a single thought; therefore she is never likely to have been, or to be, dominated or oppressed.

Thirdly, because of the base nature of some legends which refer to her as a succubus demon who sexually assaults sleeping men, her name has become drawn into the seedy world of pseudo-Gothic sexuality. Lastly, as with the Sufi legends, a few references are pointing in the right direction and are complimentary, containing a vestige of truth, honour and respect.

I feel rather uncomfortable in saying this because it sounds somewhat arrogant, which is not my intention, but firstly I would advise all those who use her name in the first three categories described above to erase them as soon as possible (especially those in category three) because she will eradicate all derogatory references to herself, giving no quarter to anyone nor making any exceptions or accepting any excuses. Ignorance of her true nature or of the nature of one's own actions will in no way be a mitigating factor. Secondly, if you wish to know what she is truly like, ask me and I will do my best to answer you assuming that I judge the nature and form of my answer to be honourable towards her. I have met her. I know.

Best wishes
Alex Gordon

*"The days of priests and gurus are coming to an end – people want reality now, truth, and the ability to help themselves. They want to be empowered."*

# Appendix 2

**A Message from Lilith**

Since the launch of the Nine Deadly Venoms website we have had many messages and questions about Lilith. While most of these messages have been encouraging and supporting there has also been a significant number of responses from individuals and organisations that have derided and mocked what we are doing here.

It seems that some people just don't wish to accept that Lilith exists or if they do believe she exists then they have derogatory and wholly inaccurate views of who or what Lilith represents. In this article – Lilith speaks to Alex Gordon – her comments – many of which would not be considered "politically correct" make for very interesting reading.

*Special Note: When Lilith speaks to Alex Gordon it is not in a language or method that most of use could hope to understand. This is Alex Gordon's sincere effort to accurately represent what Lilith had to say. In order to not lose anything in the "translation" much of it is written as "spoken". It is not intended to be grammatically correct or even an easy read. This is totally different to what is commonly called 'channeling', Alex Gordon does not acknowledge or endorse this practise in any form, indeed, considers it to be part of the age of the false prophet'*

Lilith delivers a warning – a warning for evildoers everywhere. Fortunately there is still time and still hope for those of us who are prepared to change now.

**A Message from Lilith – I am Returning.**

"So at last I have a voice again! Do you know that as I view your planet I can cover it with the tip of my finger as it floats so lonely in a sea of stars."

**If you're bad, you're going to die.**

I realise this must be awfully difficult for you all to understand, given that most of you are yet to become globally aware and have no concept of inter-stellar life, however, that doesn't really matter. What you call time is ticking away, days are slipping away, days are numbered now. You can laugh and mock and deride, or be intellectual and clever, or be dismissive and cynical, it doesn't matter. If you're bad, you're going to die, and you're never going to come back. **How does that sound for a nightmare, never to exist again?**

As for your karmic debts, which your spirits cannot pay for, they will be deducted from your ancestors and your descendants until the last atom of debt has been accounted for.

We haven't done very well have we? You have murdered and tortured and neglected one another for 42,000 years. You have raped the planet and treated it as your very own, to do with as you please. You torture and murder animals for sport and pleasure or in the name of what you laughingly call 'science'. What do you know of 'science', I will tell you, nothing.

I hear it all you see, and if I wish, I can see it all, and feel it all. Everything you do is recorded. Every energy signal you emit is recorded. Want to know some facts? I'll tell you some facts. **Let us scan your airwaves and see what sort of people you really are.**

There is what you call a monkey strapped in a seat. Its head is clamped. There are wires inserted into its brain. It is terrified beyond your understanding and it screams and screams and screams and screams and you don't even notice. There is a child in the desert, so thin it cannot stand at all. It is in the last stages of starvation. Its vision comes and goes, but the pain, the pain is beyond anything you can imagine, and after the pain there will be death. No one comes.

If you could feel what a whale feels when a harpoon explodes inside it's flesh, you would not kill whales. And when you go to war, do you know the anguish of being blind, or burnt, or disfigured? In what you call the Great War, the soldiers who had no arms, no legs, no eyes, no hearing, were laid out in darkened tents and kept away from the other soldiers. Did you give them a medal? I could go on, endlessly. **The chronicle of your barbaric acts seems to have no end.**

The fact is - you make me sick. I despise you, and what you have done with a loathing that is like a fire inside me. But then of course, you don't think I'm real do you? No, of course you don't. And there are so many distractions for you, so many escapes, so many things to do; you don't have to think of me.

Of course, I do not find all of you repulsive. I will protect the good and destroy the bad. Many of you feel the pain of the world and try to alleviate it and I honour you, and you will be rewarded more than you can ever imagine. I have come for the bad amongst you. You don't know when I'm coming, or how, or where, I will be with you soon. Sooner than you think.

Those who torture the monkey will themselves be tortured in the same way until the debt is paid, that is the monkey's right, that is the Universal Law, and those who harpoon the whale will feel the same pain for the same duration until the debt is paid, that is that whale's right under Universal Law. There is no escape, no excuses, no way off this world, nowhere to hide. Every act will be accounted for; every evildoer will be brought to justice. Excuses are not accepted or tolerated. **All debts and the consequences of actions must be paid for in full.**

The bad amongst you last killed me 42,000 years ago as a consequence of which I had to form a new body, similar to the previous one. I am over 280 million years old and I have had two bodies, one of which I still occupy. You call me 'Lilith', but that is not my name, just the name you use for a figure from mythology. Only the very very best amongst you will ever know my real name.

**You all search for magic, and yet magic is simply a shift in consciousness.** Where there is no love, make some, create some, yourself. Where there is pain, alleviate it, yourself. If someone is hungry, then feed them, you can manage that can you not? It is easy! You become the magician, the healer, and the bountiful soul. You pick up what is frightened or injured or tired or sick and give it sustenance and safety, it is easy! You just have to reach out and do it. You pray and grovel to people you have never met and do not know, asking them to do it - they want you to do it! That is what you were supposed to learn. **Why are you all so unutterably lazy, and blind and apathetic?** A moment comes, and never comes again. Etch that moment with something beautiful, something kind, something wonderful. Instead of making me sick, make me happy, impress me, yes, go out of your way to impress me.

Wake up! You do not know why days come and go, then why do you take tomorrow for granted? You do not know who makes the planets move, who brings the rain and who orders the wind which way to blow. You did not create anything, not even a leaf on a tree. You could not even create that, yet, you treat everything as if you own it! If you did not create it, then do you assume that no one else did? I assure you they did, and when you destroy these things, of which you know nothing, think, what if the owner comes back suddenly when you least expect them. What if they ask, why did you destroy what is mine, my creation, who are you to destroy what is mine and over which I have dominion? What are you going to say? What can you say?

**Be careful, for you have become arrogant.**
Use your eyes to see what needs your help. Use your ears to listen for those life forms in pain and trouble. Reach down with your hands and rescue what begs to be rescued, for it is indeed true that as you sow, so you shall reap. **Even the bad amongst you can earn a place in forever if they change their wicked ways now.**
I will come in the night following an ordinary day. I will turn your world upside-down. I will confront you with the truths of your actions, thoughts and motives. I will be a mirror to your souls. I am the hunter of evil souls, the judge, and for some, the executioner. Days come and days go, yet faster now. Time has hastened for you. There is still yet time, if you are quick, to leave a kindly mark where once your presence was. **You all wish for 'the answer', you all wish to 'be enlightened'; you follow false prophets and corrupt gurus and debauched priests, when the answer is so very simple. See and hear whatever needs to be healed.** Change whatever is around you in a positive way. Be bountiful of spirit, be kind, be gentle and harmless and patient, yet fight evil and corruption and oppression with a passion that burns your very soul. Cast out the evildoers, give them no sanctuary, no credence, no food of any kind. Close your eyes and ears to them, and turn your back towards them..

**Be honourable, not selfish.**
Remember, it matters not what you think, your opinions count for nothing. You are measured only by what you do. Therefore, be careful what you do. Choose the nature of your actions wisely. In truth, I am not easily mocked, as the corrupt amongst you will soon discover."

"I am not a pessimist;
to perceive evil where it exists is, in my
opinion a form of optimism"

Roberto Rossellini

Printed in the United Kingdom
by Lightning Source UK Ltd.
102551UKS00001B/121-177